New Directions for
Student Services

John H. Schuh
EDITOR-IN-CHIEF

Elizabeth J. Whitt
ASSOCIATE EDITOR

Addressing the Unique Needs of Latino American Students

Anna M. Ortiz

EDITOR

Number 105 • Spring 2004
Jossey-Bass
San Francisco

ADDRESSING THE UNIQUE NEEDS OF LATINO AMERICAN STUDENTS
Anna M. Ortiz (ed.)
New Directions for Student Services, no. 105
John H. Schuh, Editor-in-Chief
Elizabeth J. Whitt, Associate Editor

NEW DIRECTIONS FOR STUDENT SERVICES (ISSN 0164-7970, e-ISSN 1536-0695) is part of The Jossey-Bass Higher and Adult Education Series and is published quarterly by Wiley Subscription Services, Inc., A Wiley Company, at Jossey-Bass, 989 Market Street, San Francisco, California 94103-1741. Periodicals Postage Paid at San Francisco, California, and at additional mailing offices. POSTMASTER: Send address changes to New Directions for Student Services, Jossey-Bass, 989 Market Street, San Francisco, California 94103-1741.

New Directions for Student Services is indexed in College Student Personnel Abstracts and Contents Pages in Education.

Microfilm copies of issues and articles are available in 16mm and 35mm, as well as microfiche in 105mm, through University Microfilms Inc., 300 North Zeeb Road, Ann Arbor, Michigan 48106-1346.

SUBSCRIPTIONS cost $75.00 for individuals and $160.00 for institutions, agencies, and libraries. See ordering information page at end of book.

EDITORIAL CORRESPONDENCE should be sent to the Editor-in-Chief, John H. Schuh, N 243 Lagomarcino Hall, Iowa State University, Ames, Iowa 50011

Jossey-Bass Web address: www.josseybass.com

CONTENTS

EDITOR'S NOTES

There is little doubt that Latinos have and will continue to have a significant impact on higher education as they become the largest nonwhite ethnic group in the United States. Most Latinos in higher education have overcome economic, educational, and language barriers in order to succeed. Their presence causes us in the higher education community to reconsider our basic assumptions as we construct learning environments and opportunities that allow all students to participate fully. For instance, because over half of all Latino students are attending college in community colleges, four-year institutions have had to work more closely with community colleges to develop articulation agreements and programs that promote transfer. Because many Latino students are first-generation college students, many colleges have begun to include families and communities in orientation processes and programs. There are also countless examples of bridge programs in which students, faculty, and staff from four-year institutions work with middle schools and high schools to guide Latino students into higher education. Traditional practice in higher education has seldom made efforts like these a priority. Our common practice has assumed that students are independent of their families (or should be), that good students will find their way to college largely on their own, and that student services initiatives that work for one ethnic group will work for all.

This sourcebook explores the experiences of Latinos in higher education and seeks to shape a picture of their participation that is representative of the diversity of the group and of the higher education institutions they inhabit. The primary purpose of this sourcebook is to provide information that will be useful to the student affairs professionals that serve Latinos on a regular basis. The overarching goal is that the insight conferred by the contributing authors will have a direct impact on practice and thus the improvement of our institutions in their efforts to serve this unique and growing population of students. The sourcebook is also intended to be a resource for faculty and students in professional preparation programs as they ready themselves to serve student populations that will increasingly include Latinos of various national origins.

The authors who have contributed their work to this volume represent the future of research on Latinos in higher education. These innovative scholars all have a base of experience as practitioners that enhances their approach to research. Thus, these chapters have a blend of the most current research trends and perspectives that can be used to improve the practice of student services professionals.

In Chapter One, Vasti Torres provides an overview of the various ethnic groups that are a part of the Latino population in the United States. Often discussions of Latinos are limited to those who are of Mexican heritage. This chapter explores the experiences of other Latinos in higher education, including sociohistorical factors that affect their college experiences.

In Chapter Two, Kenneth González, Jennifer Jovel, and Carla Stoner explore the unique experiences of Latinas in higher education, emphasizing the impact of gender role expectations on Latinas' college experiences and highlighting the support that Latinas need from student services personnel.

Boualoy Dayton, Nancy Gonzalez-Vasquez, Carla Martinez, and Caryn Plum share the findings from their recent study of Hispanic-serving institutions in Chapter Three. Hispanic-serving institutions have led the nation in providing excellent student services and support programs for Latino students. This chapter explores the unique nature of these student services divisions, focusing on organizational effectiveness and the way in which their unique missions are infused in student affairs functional areas.

Theoretical considerations and their practical application are explored by Octavio Villalpando in Chapter Four. Villalpando's discussion of critical race theory challenges practitioners to consider student behavior and achievement in relation to power hierarchies and institutional oppression at predominantly white higher education institutions. This chapter provides a lens through which to examine this dynamic and strategies that can be used to help institutions to evaluate policies, practices, and procedures that negatively "serve" Latino students.

In Chapter Five, Magadelena Martinez and Edith Fernandez address the community college as the context in which the majority of Latinos enter higher education. Latino students attend community colleges in higher proportions than any other ethnic group. This chapter explores the ways in which community colleges help Latino and Latina students to achieve their educational and occupational goals, including strategies and programs that integrate family, community, and K–12 school systems.

In Chapter Six, Linda Gross addresses theoretical concerns in her study of the career decision-making process in Latino business students. She describes a process that involves a complex interplay among individual aspirations, family expectations, and peer influence that often results in considerable stress for students as they balance a myriad of expectations and their own skills and abilities.

The volume concludes with two chapters that highlight the findings and recommendations of the chapters in the volume. In Chapter Seven, three recent college graduates—José Cabrales, Cynthia Juarez, and Fernando Vasquez—and their graduate mentor, Liliana Mina, share narratives that highlight the critical role that student services programs and professionals played in their college success. Finally, in the concluding chapter, I synthesize the findings of the volume and translate them into concrete recommendations on how to improve the services and support we provide to Latinos in our institutions.

Anna M. Ortiz
Editor

ANNA M. ORTIZ is associate professor of student development in higher education at California State University, Long Beach.

1

*Research on Latino college students is largely based on
the experiences of Mexican Americans. In this chapter,
diverse experiences of other groups in terms of
immigration, educational achievement, and economic
attainment are highlighted, and implications for student
services are explored.*

The Diversity Among Us:
Puerto Ricans, Cuban Americans,
Caribbean Americans, and Central
and South Americans

Vasti Torres

Much of the research literature in higher education uses the broad terms of
Latinos or *Hispanics*, but in reality much of the literature that uses those
terms is based on the Mexican American experience. Although this research
can be translated to those from other countries, it is important to recognize
the diversity among us, to examine within-group differences and consider
how they affect the college experience for students from different countries
of origin.

The focus on Mexican Americans is justified, because between 58.5
(Guzman, 2000) and 66.1 percent (Therrien and Ramirez, 2000) of the
Latino population in the United States is of Mexican origin. The second-
largest group of U.S. Latinos (9.6 percent) claim Puerto Rico as their country of origin (not including those who remain in Puerto Rico—a U.S.
territory). The next largest group from a single country is from Cuba (4 percent of the U.S. Latino population). Other countries of origin are grouped
into geographic regions, with Central and South America represented by
14.5 percent of the population and "other Hispanic origins," which would
include other Caribbean countries, representing 6.4 percent (Therrien and
Ramirez, 2000, p. 1).

What is shared among these countries of origin is a legacy of Spanish
colonization and subsequent establishment of the Spanish language over
indigenous languages, which provide a basic link between peoples, resulting in a common group identity (Fitzpatrick, 1971). Beyond language,

New Directions for Student Services, no. 105, Spring 2004 © Wiley Periodicals, Inc.

Latinos share a sense of community and a dedication to family (Langdon and Clark, 1993). However, these commonalities often overshadow distinct immigration patterns, varying ethnic experiences in the United States, and research findings that are different for particular ethnic groups.

Immigration

The first issue that affects an immigrant group from any country is the reason for the migration. The main issues tend to be either political or economic, and each category has distinct laws, norms, and reactions within the United States. Those who migrate for political reasons have a hope of returning to their country and are called *refugees* (Levine, 1987b). Those who leave for economic reasons seek out financial opportunities, often giving up the social status they held in their country of origin; these migrants are called *immigrants* (Levine, 1987b).

Whether the migration is economic or political, it often consists of three stages, a pattern that can be referred to as the *theory of household migration* (Palmer, 1990). In the first stage, one individual (or family, in the case of political refugees) migrates to the receiving country to investigate new opportunities. The second stage begins when the migrant is settled and begins to send funds to the family remaining in the country of origin, a procedure that is referred to as *remittances*. The third stage occurs when the family is reunified in the new country. As long as other members of the extended family remain in the country of origin, remittances to the country of origin are likely to continue (Palmer, 1990). This pattern of migration is reflected in the immigration policies of the country of origin and the United States. For instance, individuals in the United States are eligible to sponsor nuclear and extended family members who wish to migrate by demonstrating financial support. Likewise, countries of origin may permit migration in efforts to unite families. It is important to understand this pattern because despite differences in the immigration stories of Latinos depending on country, region, and U.S. policy toward the country of origin, most of the stories include family reunification and financial assistance to those left behind. The following sections provide some insight into the immigration issues of Caribbean Americans and Central and South Americans.

Puerto Rican Migration: A Commuter Nation. The term *commuter nation* is used by Carlos Antonio Torre (1994) to describe the ability of Puerto Ricans to exercise their right as U.S. citizens to travel to and from the U.S. mainland in order to follow economic trends and to increase "the solidarity among the various generations of migrants" (p. 16). The migration of Puerto Ricans to the U.S. mainland began in the early twentieth century but blossomed after World War II, peaking in the 1950s with an average of 40,000 Puerto Ricans migrating annually (Levine, 1987a). By 1980, 40 percent of all people of Puerto Rican origin were residing on the U.S. mainland (Levine, 1987a).

Economic reasons have been the principal motivation for the movement to the mainland. This conclusion is confirmed by the fact that emigration rates tend to drop during recessions on the mainland (Levine, 1987a). The early migrants were mainly urban dwellers and were likely to settle in New York City. One reason for this may have been the low airfares between New York and Puerto Rico after World War II. As in other immigrant groups, after the initial migrants experienced success, others followed their example (Levine, 1987a). In the 1960s, the poem "Jet Neorriqueño" by Jaime Carrero referenced this phenomenon (García Passalacqua, 1994, p. 105). This term—Neoricans—was popularized to represent those who have been brought up in New York and are Puerto Rican. The ability to commute easily between the mainland United States and the island of Puerto Rico gives Puerto Ricans a unique ability to remain connected with their country of origin (García Passalacqua, 1994) and maintain close family ties between generations that live on the mainland and others that continue to live on the island.

Cuban Migration: Three Unique Waves. Although many think of Cuban migration as political in nature, as each wave of emigration separated family members, the political issues became intertwined with efforts toward family reunification (Bach, 1987). The emigration of Cubans was sparked by the revolution of 1959, led by Fidel Castro. At first, emigration was unrestricted, but only those with wealth tended to migrate out of Cuba. Following a series of land and legal reforms that supported the distribution of wealth and resources characteristic of communist economies, the larger-scale exodus began in 1960. Those who emigrated between 1959 and 1962 were mainly professional, managerial, and middle-class people (Bach, 1987). Compared with the overall Cuban population, this first wave of emigrants was educated, with 36 percent having completed high school or some college, in comparison to only 4 percent of the overall Cuban population having this level of education. Those in this wave of refugees were considered the "golden exiles" because of their education and wealth (Bach, 1987, p. 112).

This first wave was stopped as a result of the 1962 Cuban missile crisis. Though some continued to emigrate, the second major wave of emigrants did not begin till 1965, when the Cuban government allowed those with family in the United States to emigrate. The orderly departures from the island were carried out on "freedom flights" and were primarily restricted to emigration involving reunification of families (Bach, 1987, p. 113). By the time the freedom flights ended in 1973, more than 250,000 Cubans had been flown to the U.S. entry point of Miami. This controlled emigration allowed prior screening of emigrants by both governments. During this wave of emigration, the social class of the refugees changed; more were skilled workers, with only 18 percent considered professionals, managers, or technical workers (Bach, 1987). During this period, many who wanted to go to the United States but were not allowed to chose to leave

Cuba through Spain or other countries in hopes of entering the United States later.

The third major wave of emigrants came in 1980, when the Mariel boatlift brought 125,000 Cubans to the United States. This wave of emigrants was very diverse and included those seeking reunification who were sought out by Cuban families in the United States as well as those whom the Cuban government considered undesirables (Bach, 1987, p. 115). The emphasis on the term *undesirable* and the riots that resulted because of the conditions under which these emigrants were held created a belief that this wave of emigrants was less educated and of lower social status. This has turned out to be untrue. Later analysis of the educational and skill level of these emigrants has shown that this wave of exiles was similar in educational and occupational backgrounds to both the first and second waves (Bach, 1987).

The U.S. attitude toward the Cuban government has allowed Cubans to enter as political exiles rather than economic immigrants, offering this group privileges experienced by very few from Latin American countries. The fact that it is easier for Cubans than those from other Latin American countries to immigrate to the United States has caused tension between Cuban immigrants and those from other countries who would like to reunite their own families (Bach, 1987). This status as political exiles has also allowed Cubans more services and protection than other immigrants from Central or South America.

Dominicans. Immigrants from the Dominican Republic have tended to come largely for economic reasons. Until 1961, control over the exit visa needed to leave the county was held by the dictator Rafael Trujillo. After the assassination of Trujillo the migration of Dominicans "began in significant numbers" (Bray, 1987, p. 152). Many of those immigrants who came to the United States declared New York City as their destination, but many have also settled in New England states such as Massachusetts, Connecticut, and Rhode Island (Bray, 1987).

Central and South Americans. The countries that compose Central and South America have very different migration patterns and reasons for migration. Though economic issues are frequently associated with these countries, wars or military actions in Nicaragua, El Salvador, Guatemala, and Panama have also provided reasons to seek exile in the United States (Gugliotta, 1987). Countries with relatively stable governments, such as Costa Rica, Honduras, Belize, and most South American countries, still experience economic crises that prompt emigration to the United States in search of financial opportunities. Because much of the data reported is aggregated, it is difficult to provide in-depth information for each of the Central or South American countries represented by immigrants living in the United States.

Demographic Information on Latinos from the Caribbean and Central and South America

Latinos from the Caribbean and South and Central America also differ in their experiences in the United States. The size of the populations varies significantly, as does their economic and educational attainment, including college participation rates.

Population. It is estimated that somewhere between 33.9 percent (Therrien and Ramirez, 2000) and 41.5 percent (Guzman, 2000) of Latinos in the United States are from countries other than Mexico. The 2000 U.S. Census was the first to ask specific questions about country of origin for those self-identifying as Latino. One of the interesting issues that emerged is that the next largest group of Latinos after Mexicans was those labeled "other Hispanic" because they "did not specify a detailed Hispanic origin, but either checked the Spanish/Hispanic/Latino box . . . or wrote in answers such as 'Hispanic' or 'Latino' or 'Spanish'" (Guzman, 2000, p. 2). As previously mentioned, Puerto Ricans with 9.6 percent and Cubans with 3.5 percent are the next two largest groups of Latinos in the United States, followed by the Dominicans with 2.2 percent of the overall Latino population (Guzman, 2000). Those from Central America (not including Mexico) compose 4.8 percent of the overall population, with those from El Salvador forming the largest group (1.9 percent of the overall Latino population). Following El Salvador is Guatemala with 1.1 percent, while the other countries each account for less than 1 percent of the overall Latino population in the United States (Guzman, 2000). Among the 3.8 percent of U.S. Latinos from South America, Colombians are the largest group, accounting for 1.3 percent of the overall U.S. Latino population. After Colombia, those from Ecuador and Peru each represent 0.7 percent of the overall Latino population in the United States (Guzman, 2000).

Economic Attainment. Although most immigrants move to the United States for economic reasons, Latinos continue to lag behind non-Latino whites in economic attainment. Among Latinos who are full-time, year-round workers, only 23.3 percent earn $35,000 or more. Cuban Americans have the largest percentage (34.4 percent) of workers earning $35,000 or more, but they are still significantly behind the 49.3 percent of non-Latino whites who earn this income (Therrien and Ramirez, 2000).

An additional indicator of economic attainment is the percentage of people living below the poverty level. Among U.S. Latinos, Puerto Ricans have the largest percentage of people living below the poverty level, with 25.8 percent. The difference between the percentage of U.S. Latinos (22.8 percent) and the percentage of U.S. non-Latino whites (7.7 percent) living below the poverty level is significant and indicates the continued economic struggle of Latinos in the United States (Therrien and Ramirez, 2000).

Figure 1.1. Percentage of U.S. Population with at Least a High School Education, 2000

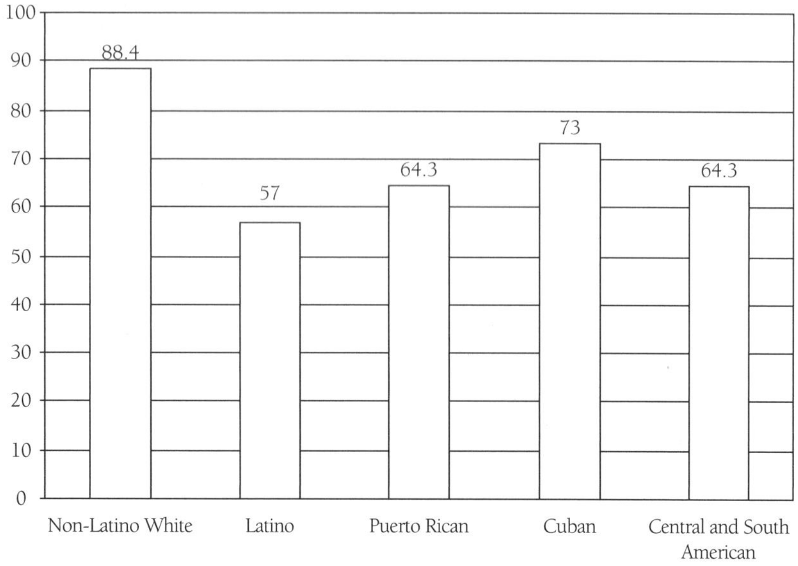

Source: Therrien and Ramirez, 2000, p. 5. © 2000 by the U.S. Census Bureau.

Educational Attainment. While many in society would consider graduation from high school to be a minimal educational attainment in today's economy, there continues to be a large gap between Latinos and non-Latino whites with regard to completion of high school. Figure 1.1 illustrates the gap in educational attainment between the 57 percent of U.S. Latinos and the 88.4 percent of U.S. non-Latino whites who have attained a high school education. Among U.S. Latinos, Cubans (73 percent) are most likely to have at least a high school education, while Mexican Americans (51 percent) are the least likely. It should be noted that the statistic of 64.3 percent of Central and South Americans with a high school education does not include Mexicans. The reasons for the gap between Latinos and non-Latino whites and Mexican Americans are complex and include timing and circumstances of migration (especially when comparing Mexicans and other Latinos), type of schooling available, socioeconomic status, and other societal issues such as quality of housing, the availability of social services, and working conditions. For all Latinos to succeed and attend higher education, the reasons for this gap must be addressed (Therrien and Ramirez, 2000).

The percentage of U.S. Latinos with a high school education influences the ability of Latinos to attend higher education institutions. Many Latinos experience difficult academic situations and therefore may not feel they

**Figure 1.2. Percentage of U.S. Undergraduates
Studying at Community Colleges, 2000**

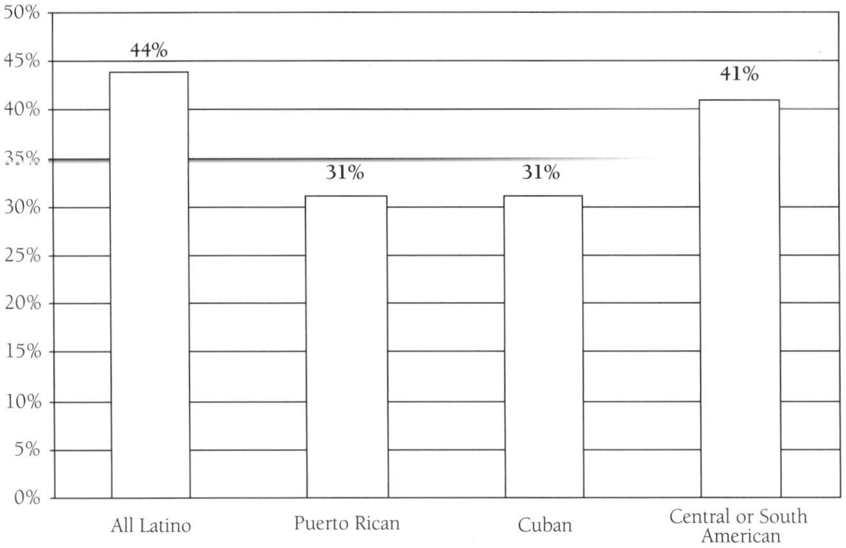

Source: Fry, 2002, p. 5. © 2002 by the Pew Hispanic Center.

hâve as many choices for higher education as other groups. The largest percentage of U.S. Latinos (44 percent) begin their higher education experience in a community college (see Figure 1.2). This trend seems to be more prevalent among Central and South American students (not including Mexicans) (41 percent) than among Puerto Rican (31 percent) or Cuban American (31 percent) students (Fry, 2002).

Enrollment information for traditional-age Latino students (18–24 years) in 2000 indicates that Cuban Americans have the highest percentage (41.7 percent) of high school graduates who enrolled in undergraduate higher education, while 28.8 percent of Puerto Rican and 37.2 percent of Central and South American high school graduates (not including Mexicans) enrolled in undergraduate higher education (Fry, 2002, p. 18). The overall percentage of Latino traditional-age high school graduates who enroll in undergraduate higher education is 33 percent (Fry, 2002). Generational status (number of generations of residence in the United States) also plays a role in predicting enrollment in higher education (Torres, 2003). Students who belong to the first generation of their family to live in the United States (foreign-born) are less likely than those in the second or third generation in the United States to enroll in college (Fry, 2002). These data illustrate the need for more outreach to Latino high

Table 1.1. College Participation of U.S. Latino Groups, by Country of Origin (percentages)

Age and Type of College	Puerto Rican	Cuban	Central or South American	All Latinos
18 to 24 years				
Two-year college	31.6	31.0	39.6	41.6
Four-year college	65.7	62.1	54.1	53.6
Graduate school	2.7	6.9	6.3	4.8
Total	100.0	100.0	100.0	100.0
25 to 34 years				
Two-year college	28.3	19.3	21.1	35.5
Four-year college	47.7	39.3	45.7	43.5
Graduate school	24.0	41.4	33.2	21.0
Total	100.0	100.0	100.0	100.0
35 years and over				
Two-year college	24.3	29.1	36.5	39.4
Four-year college	19.1	20.3	27.1	31.8
Graduate school	56.6	50.6	36.4	28.8
Total	100.0	100.0	100.0	100.0
All ages				
Two-year college	29.6	29.3	35.1	40.2
Four-year college	54.5	48.2	46.8	47.9
Graduate school	15.9	22.5	18.1	11.9
Total	100.0	100.0	100.0	100.0
In public college (percentage of all college participants)	73.3	81.7	83.5	84.5
Enrolled full-time (percentage of all college participants in age group)				
18 to 24 years	82.2	89.0	76.7	74.2
25 to 34 years	40.3	57.8	45.0	40.8
35 years and older	13.6	32.4	18.5	30.8
All ages	61.1	71.5	58.8	60.4
Undergraduates older than age 24 (percentage of total college participants)	34.1	27.9	33.6	32.2

Source: Fry, 2002, p. 21. ©2002 by the Pew Hispanic Center.

school students, especially to those who are first generation in the United States, in order to help them enter higher education.

Additional enrollment data illustrate that traditional-age students from the Caribbean and Central and South America (not including Mexico) are likely to attend four-year institutions (see Table 1.1). However, students aged thirty-five and older are more likely to attend two-year colleges. In contrast to prevailing myths about Latino students, it is important to note that the majority of traditional-age Latino students (74.2 percent) attend

Figure 1.3. Level of Education Completed for Selected Latino Immigrants to the United States

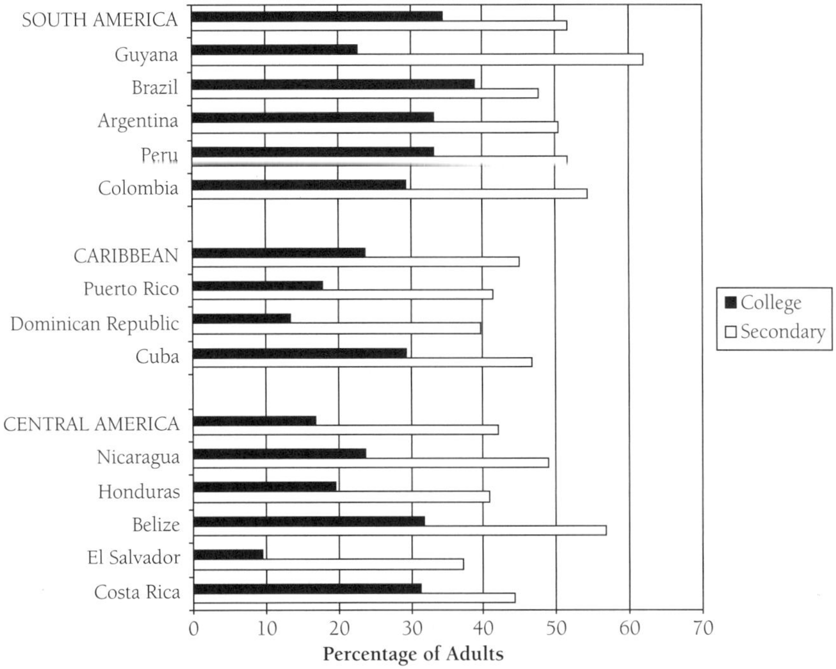

Source: Lowell and Suro, 2002, p. 10. © 2002 by the Pew Hispanic Center.

full-time. This percentage increases when you consider Puerto Rican students (82.2 percent), Cuban American students (89 percent), and Central or South American students (76.7 percent) (Fry, 2002).

College completion rates for Latino immigrants are an indicator of future economic advantage. There are significant differences among immigrants from various countries and regions (see Figure 1.3). South American immigrants are most likely to complete college, with over 30 percent having completed a bachelor's degree. The immigrants from Central America (not including Mexico) are the least likely to complete college education, with less than 20 percent possessing a bachelor's degree. An analysis of the countries of origin reveals that those who have migrated from Brazil, Argentina, and Peru are the most likely to have completed a college degree (Lowell and Suro, 2002).

These data illustrate that Latinos continue to lag behind other racial or ethnic groups in their educational attainment and that students from Caribbean and Central American countries are the most likely to experience difficulties in completing college degrees. Low educational attainment also limits the economic level that these populations can achieve.

The relationship between educational achievement and economic attainment makes educational attainment a critical issue for the U.S. Latino population in the years to come.

Current Research

The demographic information previously discussed is the most detailed information available on these groups of students. Many researchers have wondered about intragroup differences, yet few studies have sufficient numbers of students from the various countries of origin to do comparisons that would be meaningful. The College Board attempted to investigate differences among Mexican Americans, Puerto Ricans, and Cuban Americans by identifying and targeting regions where these students could be found (Pennock-Román, 1990). Some differences were found, but it was difficult to distinguish whether those differences were "associated with institutional characteristics or Hispanic subgroup membership" (p. 58). The results do suggest that Cuban American students are more likely than Mexican American or Puerto Rican students to achieve in college (Pennock-Román, 1990), which is also illustrated by generational status (successive generations are more highly educated) and other demographic variables (for example, high school graduation rates or socioeconomic status). Conducting comparison studies to minimize interactional effects of institutional differences is difficult because institutions would need large samples of students from the top three countries of origin.

Implications for Student Affairs

Perhaps the most important lesson that these statistics can teach student affairs practitioners is that students from different Latino countries have different issues. As practitioners look at the Latino population on their campus, a series of questions should be considered:

What countries are represented within the Latino population on campus? As is evident in the previous sections, students from Central America are less likely to complete a college education and may need more assistance in order to have a successful experience. If the college environment has few Latino students, it may be easy to assume they are all alike. Migration patterns from the country of origin, economic level, and parents' educational level all play a role in the experiences of these students and in understanding their needs. Data shared in this chapter illustrates that there is much diversity among Latinos.

What is the generational status of the Latino population on campus? Both quantitative (Fry, 2002) and qualitative data (Torres, 2003) illustrate that students who are first generation in United States struggle with a variety of issues within the college environment. The numbers indicate that foreign-born students are less likely to enroll in college (Fry, 2002), thus requiring institutions to provide additional recruitment and academic support if they wish to serve greater numbers of these students. Other studies have found that first-generation students deal with different cultural issues and thus need additional support (Torres, 2003). Without this additional support these students may not succeed.

Within campus programs, is there an opportunity for all countries of origin to share their own culture? This particular issue can be tricky. Although some campuses struggle with fragmented student groups, it is important to not squeeze all students into one "Latino" mold. Each of the countries of origin within the Latino label has different customs, traditional dress, and food, so it is inappropriate to assume that all Latino food is the same. Reflection on the assumptions that underlie campus programming is of paramount importance.

Conclusion

It is clear from the information presented in this chapter that much more research is needed on the diversity within the Latino population in the United States. This research also illustrates that there are common issues that cause most Latinos to lag behind non-Latino whites in both educational and economic attainment. As practitioners assess the Latino population on their own campus, it is important to understand what we have in common as well as the diversity among us.

References

Bach, R. L. "The Cuban Exodus: Political and Economic Motivations." In B. B. Levine (ed.), *The Caribbean Exodus*. New York: Praeger, 1987.

Bray, D. B. "The Dominican Exodus: Origins, Problems, Solutions." In B. B. Levine (ed.), *The Caribbean Exodus*. New York: Praeger, 1987.

Fitzpatrick, J. P. *Puerto Rican Americans: The Meaning of Migration to the Mainland.* Upper Saddle River, N.J.: Prentice Hall, 1971.

Fry, R. *Latinos in Higher Education: Many Enroll, Too Few Graduate.* Washington, D.C.: Pew Hispanic Center, 2002. [http://www.pewhispanic.org/site/docs/pdf/latinosin highereducation-sept5–02.pdf]. Accessed Jan. 20, 2004.

García Passalacqua, J. M. "The Puerto Ricans: Migrants or Commuters?" In C. A. Torre (ed.), *The Commuter Nation: Perspectives on Puerto Rican Migration.* Rio Piedras: Universidad de Puerto Rico, 1994.

Gugliotta, G. "The Central American Exodus: Grist for the Migrant Mill." In B. B. Levine (ed.), *The Caribbean Exodus.* New York: Praeger, 1987.

Guzman, B. *The Hispanic Population: Census 2000 Brief.* Current Population Reports, C2KBR/01–3. Washington, D.C.: U.S. Census Bureau, 2000.

Langdon, H. W., and Clark, L. W. "Profile of Hispanic/Latino American Students." In L. W. Clark and D. E. Waltzman, (eds.), *Faculty and Student Challenges in Facing Cultural and Linguistic Diversity.* Springfield, Ill.: Charles C. Thomas, 1993.

Levine, B. B. "The Puerto Rican Exodus: Development of the Puerto Rican Circuit." In B. B. Levine (ed.), *The Caribbean Exodus.* New York: Praeger, 1987a.

Levine, B. B. "Surplus Populations: Economic Migrants and Political Refugees." In B. B. Levine (ed.), *The Caribbean Exodus.* New York: Praeger, 1987b.

Lowell, B. L., and Suro, R. *The Improving Educational Profile of Latino Immigrants.* Washington, D.C.: Pew Hispanic Center, 2002. [http://www.pewhispanic.org/site/docs/pdf/ImmigEd12–04–02Final2.pdf]. Accessed Jan. 20, 2004.

Palmer, R. W. *In Search of a Better Life: Perspectives on Migration From the Caribbean.* New York: Praeger, 1990.

Pennock-Román, M. *Test Validity and Language Background: A Study of Hispanic American Students at Six Universities.* New York: College Board Publications, 1990.

Therrien, M., and Ramirez, R. R. *The Hispanic Population in the United States: March 2000.* Current Population Reports, P20–535. Washington, D.C.: U.S. Census Bureau, 2000.

Torre, C. A. "Victims of the Knight: An Introduction to the Commuter Nation." In C. A. Torre (ed.), *The Commuter Nation: Perspectives on Puerto Rican Migration.* Rio Piedras: Universidad de Puerto Rico, 1994.

Torres, V. "Influences on Ethnic Identity Development of Latino College Students in the First Two Years of College." *Journal of College Student Development,* 2003, 44(4), 532–547.

VASTI TORRES is associate professor of higher education and student affairs at Indiana University.

2

The numbers of Latinas who attend college, stay in college, graduate, and attend graduate school escalated in the 1990s, surpassing gains made by any other underrepresented group of students in higher education. However, their achievements come at a personal cost, as the high-achieving Latinas profiled in this chapter demonstrate.

Latinas: The New Latino Majority in College

Kenneth P. González, Jennifer E. Jovel, Carla Stoner

Quizá la culpa es mía
Por no seguir la norma
Ya es demasiado tarde
Para cambiar ahora
Me mantendré firme en mis convicciones
Reforzare mis posiciones
Mí destino es el que yo
Decido el que yo
Elijo para mí

Perhaps it is my fault
for not following the norm
It's too late now to change anything
I will stand firm by my convictions
reinforce my position
My destiny is what I choose
the one I choose for me
—Thalia, "¿A Quién le Importa?" 2002

Historically, the roles of Latinas were limited to the home environment. They were viewed as daughters, mothers, wives, and nothing more. Over the last two decades, however, their image has changed. Latinas are taking their lives into their own hands, leaving behind the expectations of the past. They have defined a new set of convictions and are walking toward destinies of their own choosing. This chapter explores the growing presence of Latinas in higher education and the challenges and sacrifices accompanying their progress.

NEW DIRECTIONS FOR STUDENT SERVICES, no. 105, Spring 2004 © Wiley Periodicals, Inc.

Latinas: A Growing Presence

During the last decades of the twentieth century, it was predicted that the century ahead would be characterized by a boom in the Latino population, making Latinos the largest minority group in the United States and the majority in California. As we progress through the twenty-first century, it is evident that what preceded the new millennium was the decade of the Latina. The 1990s marked a period of significant educational advancement for Latinas. Although Latinas and Latino males both remained underrepresented in higher education, Latinas in particular increased their presence during the 1990s.

Throughout the 1980s, the percentage of eighteen- to twenty-four-year-old Latinas who enrolled in college remained at approximately 16 percent. During the 1990s, however, Latina participation in college steadily increased, and by 2000, 25.4 percent of Latinas in this age group enrolled in college. Meanwhile, Latino males experienced slower enrollment increases, from 15.3 percent in 1990 to 18.5 percent in 2000. Thus, Latinas achieved almost a 7 percent lead over Latino males in college participation (American Council on Education, 2002). Furthermore, while the college graduation rate of Latinas grew from 53.7 percent in 1990 to 65.7 percent in 2000, the graduation rate of Latino males remained nearly unchanged at 54 percent (American Council on Education, 2002). In short, Latinas surpassed their male counterparts in both college participation and completion.

The advances made by Latinas during the 1990s also are evident in the increased percentages of degrees conferred. Compared to white, African American, Asian American, and American Indian men and women, Latinas experienced the largest increase in associate and bachelor's degrees conferred. Between 1991 and 2000, the percentage of all associate and bachelor's degrees granted to Latinas grew from 5.2 percent and 3.5 percent to 9 percent and 6.3 percent, an average increase of about 75 percent for each degree (American Council on Education, 2002). Furthermore, Latinas achieved the second largest increase at the master's degree level. The percentage of all master's degrees conferred on Latinas increased 63 percent, from 2.7 percent in 1991 to 4.4 percent in 2000 (American Council on Education, 2002).

Although the overall percentages of college participation, completion, and degrees granted have remained relatively low for Latinas, the increases that took place during the 1990s reflect significant progress. Latinas' progress in higher education has been notably greater than that of Latino males and men and women of different racial/ethnic groups. Unfortunately, the gains Latinas have made in higher education have not come without significant challenges and sacrifices. Using data from a comprehensive study on Latina college students, the remainder of this chapter highlights some of the challenges that Latinas still encounter in their quest for higher education.

Challenges and Sacrifices

In the fall of 2000, we began investigating the educational experiences of Latinas in their quest for a college degree. The purpose of the study was twofold: (1) to understand the factors in expansion and constriction of college opportunities for Latinas, and (2) to disentangle the multiple strands in the issue of Latinas leaving home for college.

To focus our investigation, we used life history research methods (Dollard, 1935; Goodson, 1981) to examine the K–12 and college experiences of two different groups of Latinas. Both groups were raised in working-class home environments and attended public schools of low to middle socioeconomic status. (The term *working-class* refers to people who work for hourly wages, not salaries, especially manual or industrial laborers.) The first group of Latinas we interviewed (twelve total) completed their K–12 schooling and had the opportunity to attend two of the most selective universities in the nation. The second group of Latinas we interviewed (ten total) began their postsecondary education at a California community college. These students eventually transferred to California's most selective postsecondary institution: the University of California.

The challenges encountered by Latinas in higher education and the sacrifices they make in order to progress are many—too numerous and important to discuss in one chapter. Elsewhere we discuss at length the tensions and challenges Latinas experience during their K–12 education that threaten their opportunity for postsecondary participation (González, Stoner, and Jovel, 2003). In this chapter, we discuss the challenges and sacrifices of Latinas once they have been admitted to a highly selective four-year university. One of the first challenges experienced by the Latinas in our study was breaking the expectation that they would live at home while enrolled in college. For these women, the decision to leave home for college involved an opportunity both to better themselves and to gain a sense of independence. For example, one of the students stated:

> I knew from the beginning that I wanted to leave Southern California and my family. It was because I needed to get away from my family. I was too dependent on them. I was the youngest, and all my problems were always taken care of for me. I had six people ahead of me to turn to, plus sisters-in-law and brothers-in-law. So I remember I felt weak as a person being so dependent, and I wanted to leave. I love my family, but I just needed to go away so I could be independent.

Not all of the students in the study were the youngest in their family. But they all shared the desire to become independent. Each of them shared concerns about remaining dependent on their family and on others if they remained at or close to home.

Another student described her need for independence in this way:

> For me, it was about independence. I needed to get away so that I could grow. I needed to know what it would feel like to be on my own, to be independent. I went away before, but that was just for two weeks or so. This time, I would really be on my own. I knew it would be tough, but I also knew that's what I needed to do to grow.

Other students in the study made similar statements about their need for independence. Most of them commented that remaining at home during their college years would not have allowed them to fully develop and become independent.

Despite their desire to attend a highly selective university, there were tensions associated with their decision to leave home. In fact, only one student in the study did not experience any tension or conflict about her decision to leave home to attend college. A student who did experience tensions described her mother's reaction to her acceptance into the University of California, Berkeley:

> My mom was sad. I remember when I found out, she was in the kitchen. I said, "Mom! I got in!" And she said, "Oh, now you are leaving." And then she stayed quiet. I felt like I had to apologize, even though I was happy.

Along with their excitement about the opportunity to attend a prestigious university, many of the students commented that they carried a sense of guilt with their decision to leave home. Most of the students described the awkwardness of feeling both happy and guilty at the same time. Another student described her father's reaction:

> My dad was actually mad back then. He was really mad that I did not go to the local university. He really wanted me to go there. He was really mad that I did not even apply there. He wanted me to stay in Southern California. He wanted me to go to college, but he also wanted me to stay nearby.

At the other extreme from the students' desire to be independent and to accept a unique college opportunity was their parents' need for them to remain close to home. The students and their parents were caught in a web of conflict and opportunity. The students were aware of the contradiction. One of the students stated:

> Our father always told us, "We didn't come to the U.S. for nothing." We came here for opportunities. And here I had one of the best opportunities in the world. I think that was something he couldn't ignore.

Tensions surrounded these young women as a result of opportunities that would place them outside of their home and family environment. From our data, we came to understand that all of the parents were largely supportive of their daughters' college opportunities but did not want those opportunities to take their daughters away from the family. The students indicated that their parents wanted nothing more than better opportunities for their daughters. However, the students also commented that they did not think their parents were prepared for the kinds of opportunities that would take them away from home.

One of the more insightful findings of the study involved uncovering the roots of the parents' need for their daughters to remain close to home. One of the students captured this need in the following way:

> My mom was like, "Why do you have to move? Why can't you stay here?" She was really afraid for me more than anything else. I think she was worried about what was going to happen to me, who was going to take care of me, things like that. I think those were the greatest concerns of my parents and family.

Nearly every student in the study had something to say about their parents' concern about who would take care of them. This concern was often the primary reason why parents were apprehensive about their daughters leaving.

A second student highlighted how her parents' concern about who would take care of her was gender-specific:

> Oh yeah, the boys could do whatever they wanted. They could leave when they wanted. They did not have to go to school to leave the house. One of my brothers left the house without even being married. It was not a big deal. But for us, the only way you can leave the house is to go to school or get married. Even now, my mom feels like she is still taking care of me because I am not married. It's like, the girls have to be taken care of until there is a man to do it. It's different for the boys; they can leave the house without being married or going to school. It's because everyone thinks they can take care of themselves, but not us.

From our data, we began to uncover a belief system that most of these women confronted in their decision to leave home for college. The belief was that women are unable to take care of themselves and can only be taken care of by the parents, family, or a spouse. Leaving home without being married was only possible by going to college, but even this scenario did not provide an answer to the question "Who will take care of her?" It was difficult for the parents to believe, understand, or even consider that these women could take care of themselves.

Support Systems for Daughters. In fact, what eased the situation of these women in leaving home for college was an acquired understanding by the parents that there would be support systems within the university readily available for their daughters. For example, one of the students described the role of her sibling in her decision to leave home for college. She stated:

> I was lucky because I had a brother that went here before me. He convinced my parents that I would be okay. He told them about the kinds of support systems that would be here for me. When we came for our visit, he introduced my parents to the director of El Centro [a Chicano cultural and student center] and a Latino professor on campus. That made a big difference. My parents felt better knowing that there were Latinos here on campus that would look after me.

Three of the students in our study had an older sibling who went away to college before they did. The women described how helpful it was to have an older sibling speak with their parents about the support that would be available to them. In these cases, the siblings served as advocates, reassuring parents that their daughters would have the social and emotional support necessary to succeed in college.

Another student described the role of the church in easing the apprehension of her mother and grandmother. She commented:

> I remember when I came for my first visit to the university with my mom and my grandmother. They were still very worried about me living away from home. But once my grandma saw the beautiful church, she felt better. I guess she thought that the church would protect me in some way. I think that made my mom feel a little better too.

Another student described her parents' positive reaction when they learned that her roommate was Latina. She stated:

> One thing that really helped was that my roommate was Latina. It not only made me feel better about being here, but it also made my parents feel better. As soon as they met her, they felt better. I guessed it helped them to know that I wouldn't be here all alone, and that there were other Latinas here too.

For most of the women in the study, leaving home for college was something new to their family. As indicated earlier, parents were not prepared for the opportunities for social mobility that would take their daughters away from home. Knowing that social and emotional support systems were readily available to their daughters eased parents' apprehensions. These support systems took the form of Latino faculty and staff on campus, the presence of a church on campus, and other Latino college students.

The Sacrifices of Leaving Home for College. In further disentangling the different tensions of Latinas leaving home for college, we discovered that for many of these women, leaving home was much easier to negotiate than remaining far away from their families. In fact, every student in the study described the frustration she experienced from losing frequent contact with her family members. One of the women put it this way:

Throughout high school, I was in programs that took me away from home during the summer. So when I left for college, I was like, "Yes! I am out of here—away from my parents and away from the rules." They dropped me off; it was a little sad, but I was fine—for a little while. But then I started to miss them.So you see, the actual act of leaving home was not that difficult, it was staying away from home that was really difficult for me. The fact that I cannot just hang out with my friends or family and watch a *novela*. I really miss those things. Also, speaking Spanish, I really miss speaking Spanish.

Another student pondered whether it was her ethnic and cultural background that made it so difficult to be away from her family. She stated:

I don't know if it's because we are Mexican, but we are very close. We are a very close family. The hardest time for me here at school is when I miss them a lot. Like when I came back from spring break, I was so used to being around all of them. It's so different being away from home. It's really hard. And that's what my other friends talk about too. They're also Mexican. They hate being away from their families too.

Most students who leave home for college experience homesickness. It is a common collegiate experience. However, for the women in our study, missing family was not just a first-year college experience. It was something that bothered them throughout their college career. Another student described her experience in the following way:

I'm a junior now, and it is still hard for me to be so far away from my family. I hate knowing that there is a fiesta going on back home and I am not there. And there is one going on almost every weekend. They call or I call, and then the phone gets passed around to everyone. They say they are eating *carne asada*, and I can hear the music in the background. I miss so many things by not being there. I had a niece born while I was away at school, my second year. I wasn't even there at the hospital. I had been at the hospital for all nine of the other ones. This was the first one that I was not there. Oh, it kills me. She does not even know me when I go home. She does not recognize me. She has already started walking, and I was not there for that. But all the others, I would change their diapers; I would take care of and help raise them. I was not even there for her baptism. Stuff like that kills me. I can't go home for birthdays, or Mother's Day, or Father's Day. That's the hardest part about living so far away.

It is interesting to note that over half of the women in the study had a niece or nephew, and each of those women made it a point to share with us how difficult it was to be away from them—to not be there while they were growing up. It was clear from the data that there were sacrifices and costs of being away from home. The cost of attending a university away from home was losing contact and interaction with family members. Every woman in the study described the pain associated with these emotional costs.

In fact, the juniors and seniors in our study were experiencing great turmoil over whether they would continue to live away from home after they graduated from college. Four of the students were preparing their applications for graduate school. They knew that they might be confronted with another opportunity that would take them away from their family. Given the emotional costs of living away from home for four years, many of these women wondered whether they were willing to pay these costs again. For example, one of the students stated:

> I don't know what I am doing—because I want to go to grad school, and I am looking into the East Coast. I don't know why I do this to myself. I would be in the same situation as I am now, but on the East Coast. So I keep doing this to myself, and I keep hating it. And I don't know why I do it. I'm torn between wanting to be with my family and wanting the opportunity to further my education. It's like there's still so much more out there for me. I just wish I didn't have to be away from my family. I don't know what to do.

Another student offered a similar statement:

> I've just applied to grad school. And most of the schools I've applied to are on the East Coast. I know my parents won't be happy about me living even farther away. The thing that's different now is that part of me wants to go back home. But the other part of me wants to continue to explore what's out there. I want to know what the East Coast is like. I know that I'm going to hate being away from my family. It will be even harder for me to visit them. It's really hard, but I think I need to do this.

Most of the students indicated that their parents were expecting that they would return home after graduation. They were preparing themselves for the impending conversation. They knew that their desire to attend graduate school might send them farther away from their family. This time, unlike after high school, the students were torn between returning to their family and continuing their education at an institution far away from their family. In the end, the students felt that their parents would be supportive of whatever decision they made. This time the tension existed not between the parents and the student but within the student herself.

A Chicana Feminist Perspective

With regard to the challenges and sacrifices made by Latinas to attend college, the work of Chicana feminist scholars is instructive. These scholars have provided the academic community with a critique of the male-centered, patriarchical, and heterosexist family structure found within the

Latino community. Paula Moya (2001) suggests that the work of Chicana feminist scholars is to identify and acknowledge the conflicts and contradictions found in the Chicano community and attempt to work through them to create a qualitatively new and better social order. She defines her work with the concept of "the politics of transfiguration"—a "transformative exercise by which historically oppressed people engage in imagining the emergence of qualitatively new desires, social relations, and modes of association" (p. 459).

We argue that the young women in this study were engaged in such a process. They acknowledged the conflicts within their families by challenging not only their roles as women but also their abilities and capacities. These women not only had the courage to leave their homes despite the apprehensions of their parents but also demonstrated that they could, in fact, take care of themselves and see themselves through graduation.

The juniors and seniors in our study were in the process of imagining new social relations between themselves and their family members. They were caught between their desires to be with their family and their hopes and dreams of further discovering themselves and the world around them. On this point, we find the work of Gloria Anzaldua (1987) instructive. Anzaldua describes the ambivalence Latinas encounter as a result of belonging to more than one world. For the women in our study, these worlds encompass the Latina community, which places a high value on family and interdependence, and the predominantly white academic world, which favors the values of individuality and independence. Anzaldua (1987) argues that Latinas must refuse to remain caught in such a place of contradiction. She constructed the idea of "mestiza consciousness" to suggest that Latinas can work out a synthesis between seemingly opposing worlds. Such work, she argues, creates a reality that is "greater than the sum of its severed parts" (p. 79). Moya (2001) and Anzaldua (1987) are in agreement that the work of Latina feminists is first to imagine a better world in order to help chart the paths down which they, as Chicana feminists, are going— paths that would help them to decide what actions they should take, how they should prioritize their efforts, and whether and when they should consider changing directions.

The Role of Student Affairs Professionals

It is important for student affairs professionals to understand the experiences of all students. In this final section, we offer key insights for student affairs professionals working in a variety of functional areas. Those involved in admissions and early outreach services will note that the data presented suggest that young Latina women are eager to develop their sense of independence. These women were not only ready for college but also willing to go the distance required to attend the institution that had the best opportunities for them. Concomitantly, the data revealed the tension Latinas often experience between their desire to attend a college away from home and their parents' concern over who would take care of them. At the root of this tension is a belief system that says women cannot take care of themselves. These women knew otherwise and found ways to convince their parents that they could make it without a man or their family in close proximity. It is important to note that key aspects of the college environment eased the apprehensions of their parents. For some parents, it was knowing that their daughters had the resources and support of Latino faculty, staff, and students. For others, it was the reassurance of a sibling or the presence of a religious building. In every case, when parents made a connection with some part of the university environment that was consistent with their values and culture, apprehensions about their daughter leaving home for college diminished.

The findings of the study also offer insights for student affairs professionals supporting the development and success of students throughout their college years. Those concerned with persistence and the overall well-being of students need to consider the constant discontent that Latina women endure as a result of losing frequent personal contact with their family. Student affairs professionals need to be mindful that the collegiate experience need not be solely about individuality. In particular, it might be helpful to consider and support the ways that students develop in the context of their family relationships. For instance, financial aid packages could include funding for trips home to visit family, and student activities could include family members or be centered on the concept of family.

Finally, the data in the study provide important insights for student affairs professionals supporting students' transitions from college to graduate and professional school programs. For every women in our study, a central issue in their decision about continuing their academic development in graduate school involved whether they would return home or seek an institution that would place them even farther away from their families. Each student was caught between the desire to return home and regain her personal connections with family members and the opportunity to develop in a new and different context. None of the women had a simple answer for this dilemma. There may be no simple answers. However, the women in this study demonstrated that every step a Latina takes outside traditional expectations creates more opportunities for Latinas in the future. Student affairs professionals need not only to be aware of these difficult decisions but also to recognize the unfamiliar territory these women must negotiate. These concerns about postcollegiate options have particular relevance for student affairs units that program and advise junior and senior students who are involved in graduate school and career planning.

The results of our study have convinced us that the collegiate experience for Latinas is unique in many respects. Furthermore, we believe that it is in the best interest of all students for student affairs professionals to understand their unique backgrounds and experiences. We propose that more work needs to be done to better understand the experiences of Latinas and other underrepresented students. We encourage student affairs professionals to continue this work.

References

American Council on Education. *Nineteenth Annual Report on Minorities in Higher Education.* Washington, D.C.: American Council on Education, 2002.

Anzaldua, G. *Borderlands/La Frontera: The New Mestiza.* San Francisco: Spinsters/Aunt Lute, 1987.

Dollard, J. "Criteria for the Life History: With Analysis of Six Notable Documents." New Haven, Conn.: Yale University Press, 1935.

González, K. P., Stoner, C., and Jovel, J. "Understanding the Role of Social Capital in Access to College for Latinas: Toward a College Opportunity Framework." *Journal of Hispanic Higher Education,* 2003, 2, 146–170.

Goodson, I. "Life Histories and the Study of Schooling." *Interchange on Educational Policy,* 1981, 11, 62–76.

Moya, P.M.L. "Chicana Feminism and Postmodernist Theory." *Signs: Journal of Women in Culture and Society,* 2001, 26, 441–483.

Thalia. "¿A Quien le Importa?" On *Thalia.* (CD.) EMI Latin Records, 2002.

KENNETH P. GONZÁLEZ *is associate professor of education at the University of San Diego.*

JENNIFER E. JOVEL *is a doctoral candidate at Stanford University.*

CARLA STONER *is a student affairs officer at the University of California, Merced.*

3

Every year, more colleges and universities become Hispanic-serving institutions. These institutions, whether public or private, two-year or four-year, find themselves in the position of serving high numbers of Latino students. They encounter opportunities for unique learning environments, access to special funding, and the potential to be instrumental in Latino educational attainment.

Hispanic-Serving Institutions Through the Eyes of Students and Administrators

Boualoy Dayton, Nancy Gonzalez-Vasquez, Carla R. Martinez, Caryn Plum

Hispanic-serving institutions (HSIs) are colleges and universities with a student body that is at least 25 percent Latino (Devarics, 1998). Title V, the Developing Hispanic Serving Institutions Program of the Higher Education Act of 1965, as amended in 1993, also requires HSIs, by definition, to ensure that at least 50 percent of their Latino students are low-income individuals and that those institutions have nonprofit status (Stearns and Watanabe, 2002). Elsewhere in this volume, it has been demonstrated that Latinos are a fast-growing student population. Of U.S. Latinos enrolled in higher education, 50 percent attend a Hispanic-serving institution (Hispanic Association of Colleges and Universities, 2004). HSIs vary from two-year (52.7 percent) to four-year (47.3 percent) institutions and public (68 percent) to private institutions (32 percent) (Laden, 2001). Many of the private institutions have a religious affiliation with the Catholic Church. Over two hundred Hispanic-serving institutions are found in twelve states and Puerto Rico (Laden, 2001). States with the largest Hispanic populations have the highest numbers of HSIs; for example, as of 2001, California had fifty-seven HSIs, Puerto Rico had forty-seven, and Texas had thirty-two. However, HSIs can also be found in midwestern and eastern seaboard states (Laden, 2001). For the well-being of Hispanic populations and of society at large, it is critical to understand the important role that HSIs play in the educational advancement of Latino students.

NEW DIRECTIONS FOR STUDENT SERVICES, no. 105, Spring 2004 © Wiley Periodicals, Inc.

The purpose of this chapter is to examine the campuses of Hispanic-serving institutions through the eyes of administrators and students. We report on the findings from a study of eight administrators and fourteen students at HSIs in both California and Texas. We explore the history of the institutions and the various programs and services available at these campuses. In addition, we describe the benefits and challenges of being an HSI from the viewpoint of both students and administrators.

History of Hispanic-Serving Institutions

Hispanic-serving institutions became officially recognized through the efforts of Latino educators and business leaders dedicated to Latinos' pursuit of higher education. These leaders came together to establish the Hispanic Association of Colleges and Universities (HACU) in 1986. The mission of HACU is to improve educational access and raise the quality of college opportunities for Latinos (Laden, 2001).

HSIs are a subset of minority-serving institutions, which consist of historically black colleges and universities (HBCUs), tribal colleges and universities, and HSIs. The difference between HSIs and HBCUs and tribal colleges is that HSIs were not created to serve a specific population but evolved due to their geographic proximity to Latino populations (O'Brien, 1998). Although there are differences between the institutions, there has been constant collaboration among minority-serving institutions. From that collaboration came the Alliance for Equity in Higher Education, which consists of founding members from the National Association for Equal Opportunity in Higher Education, HACU, and the American Indian Higher Education Consortium. The alliance was formed in 1999, funded by the W. K. Kellogg Foundation, to promote "greater collaboration and cooperation among colleges and universities that serve large numbers of students of color in order to enhance the nation's economic competitiveness, social stability and cultural richness" (St. John, 1999, p. 16).

Funding of Hispanic-Serving Institutions

Federal support for Hispanic-serving institutions derived from a history and purpose unique to other minority-serving institutions. Historically black colleges and universities and tribal colleges began receiving federal support as a result of a special relationship with the government that led to federal responsibility for the welfare and education of the populations that those institutions serve (Wolanin, 1998). However, HSIs' support is not based on the same principles. Because HSIs were first predominantly white institutions, they needed to negotiate federal assistance through the leadership of HACU. The inclusion of HSIs as part of federal funding was based on the goal of "providing equal educational opportunity for all Americans" (Wolanin, 1998, p. 30) and was institutionalized through the Higher Education Act, Title III, in 1992.

This cleared the way for HSIs to access federal funding available to other minority-serving institutions (Laden, 2001). As a result, HSIs were first funded through the Higher Education Act in the 1995 fiscal year. In that year, institutions that met eligibility criteria received federal five-year development grants with the goal of helping postsecondary institutions to improve and expand their capacity to serve Hispanic and low-income students (U.S. Department of Education, "Strengthening HSIs").

In 1998, an amendment to the Higher Education Act that included Hispanic-serving institutions was placed in Title V, focusing on institutional development rather than assistance for individual students who may attend these institutions. Under this amendment, institutions could apply for and receive individual institutional development grants—funds to support cooperative agreements with other Hispanic serving institutions—as well as one-year planning grants to support future grant applications (U.S. Department of Education, "Developing HSIs Program"). The funding under this act has doubled since the year 2000 and continues to grow. In 2000, $42.5 million was awarded to institutions; for the fiscal year 2003, the estimated funding is $89.1 million (Devarics, 2002). Other funding sources for Hispanic-serving institutions can be found in such federal programs as TRIO programs, GEAR UP, the Fund for the Improvement of Postsecondary Education, and the Strengthening Institutions program (U.S. Department of Education, "1998 Amendments").

Private funding, on the other hand, can be scarce for Hispanic-serving institutions. One organization that has provided funding to help enroll and retain Hispanic students and enhance educational practice and policy on their behalf is the W. K. Kellogg Foundation. For example, in 2000, the W. K. Kellogg Foundation awarded $28 million to Hispanic-serving institutions in an effort to build coalitions among secondary schools, postsecondary institutions, community organizations, and business corporations for the purpose of improving outreach and retention efforts for Latino Americans. The goal was to build strong partnerships and develop a strategic plan for how the community as a whole can improve the educational attainment of Latino Americans. The strategies developed by the W. K. Kellogg Foundation provide a successful program model for private entities to follow. These partnerships exemplify the type of services that can help HSIs and Latino scholars become successful in the future.

The Experiences of Students and Administrators at Hispanic-Serving Institutions

Administrators and students from five public and three private four-year universities in California and Texas were interviewed to explore the experiences of working and going to college in HSI environments. The eight administrators worked in student affairs; the majority were chief student affairs officers for their campus. The number of years they had served the universities varied from one to twenty-seven years. The fourteen Latino students were of traditional college age (between the ages of eighteen and twenty-four) and ranged from first-year to senior-year status. Interviews were conducted in person when possible, but a number of interviews were conducted by telephone. Although separate protocols were used for students and administrators, both types of interviews focused on the individual's experiences in an effort to understand and explore how Hispanic-serving institutions are meeting the needs of students.

Cultural Challenges. For Latino populations, overcoming traditional cultural barriers is a common issue that many first-generation college students face. One student noted, "Most Hispanic parents don't have a high school diploma. So usually, as a Hispanic, you're the first person [in your family] to go to college." A second student talked about the level of expectations in the culture that affects college-bound Latinos: "The expectations might be different. I've seen lowered expectations here in town; sometimes that troubles me. I've come to associate that with traditional, older-generation Mexican American culture." This student was troubled by many Latinos' lack of motivation in pursuing higher education. In his own group of friends, he saw limited goals and low expectations for performing well in the university setting.

For many women, it is particularly difficult to successfully complete a college degree because of traditional cultural barriers. An administrator remarks:

> [For] Latino women, it is not seen as [more] important for them to go on and get an education than it is to develop a home. So many of them have to make great sacrifices, because they do have families, as do many of our other students, but they are expected [to do] more, to do the family-oriented piece as opposed to going on to get a doctorate, which makes things difficult for our Latino female students.

There was often a conflict between family and academic responsibilities. In Spanish terms, this is called "*familismo*, or family interdependence" (McGoldrick, Giordano, and Pearce, 1996, p. 175), which is the attitude and value of placing the interests of the family over those of the individual. One student said:

> [The university] needs to understand how important spending time with family means to me, because I spend a lot of time at school and I don't get to see my family because the way they schedule classes and some of the requirements for the class session prevents that from happening. I wish they would prevent that, or it would be great if they could have more family events. . . . [It] goes back to family and time constraint. I need to be there, and there is the expectation of our family to be there. There are times I need to be somewhere or work on a project, and family does not understand why.

They have a family orientation only during the freshman year, but once that is over with that is it.

These struggles and challenges can be seen repeatedly throughout Latino student populations in higher education. The cultural value of a strong family unit can sometimes be at odds with achieving a college degree. Many Latino students are first-generation college students who struggle to find the balance between their school and family obligations.

These cultural challenges are often reinforced by the location of Hispanic-serving institutions. Because many are located in areas with high concentrations of Latinos in the population, students can remain at home while attending college. While the family plays a key role in supporting students, as demonstrated in Chapters Two and Eight of this volume, having family close by (or in the same house) may create challenges to college achievement. Because students remain in an environment where the cultural values concerning family responsibility are continually reinforced, academic responsibilities and regular progress may be compromised.

The support and comfort that students experience while attending an institution where they feel at ease with other Latino students is commonly understood to be a benefit to students' college achievement. Students gain a valuable support system and are able to learn more about themselves in a comfortable and safe environment where they share many common experiences with their peers. A student explains:

> I was intimidated that if I went to a university, that I would be the only Hispanic in the class, making you the representative of 'your group.' [At the HSI] it's more about the individual and not so much a focus on your race. You don't feel like there's added stress or pressure because you're the only minority in the classroom.

She went on to say how that has helped her address the issue of race: "It has taught me that race is an important issue and people need to address it. That's how people view you and that's how you view the world. It's taught me to be proud of myself." Learning about race in a supportive environment has dramatically different results from learning about race in predominantly white institutions. However, one student recognized the difficulties that may arise from being in such a supportive environment when making a transition to the working world after college: "Where I work, it is mainly populated by races other than Hispanics. Being so used to working with Hispanics and going through the transition of working with people from other races is kind of difficult." Achieving a balance between promoting the supportive environment and readying students for employment in less supportive environments is also a challenge perpetually encountered by other minority-serving institutions.

Role of Faculty and Staff at HSIs. The roles of Latino faculty and staff differ from campus to campus. Administrators had different opinions on what these roles were and their impact on the campus and students. Students offered unique perspectives on whether the presence of Latino faculty and staff was of great importance in their college experiences.

An administrator at a California university voiced the importance of having faculty and staff reflect the campus demographics. Diverse faculty and staff communities were viewed as significant components in developing an institutional understanding of some of the common challenges minority students face, because they were more likely to have experienced the challenges of being a first-generation student or learning about the proverbial hoops one must jump through in order to survive in college. An institutional commitment to recruiting and retaining Latino faculty and staff was noted as a critical factor in ensuring a diverse staff that reflects the student body, because professionals who have experienced struggles similar to those of Latinos could use their personal experiences to establish a sense of understanding and support within the institution. An administrator at one campus stated, "Our institution, as well, is very reflective of the demographics, if you look at our staffing. Many of [the staff] have gone through what many of [the students] have gone through, and that's important."

At another university, Latino faculty and staff were important because they served as consultants and representatives of the campus conscience. The administrator at this campus stated that the roles of faculty and staff were crucial when dealing with political issues that arise among different Latino student organizations and in trying to fully understand the needs of Latino students. The personal insights that Latino faculty and staff offer were essential in ensuring campus sensitivity, empathy, and responsiveness to the needs and concerns of Latino students. The administrator stated:

> We work in very close consultation with Chicano/Latino faculty, particularly around issues of political sensitivity and ethnic sensitivity. They serve as the conscience and guides in terms of trying to understand the needs. So there are times of tensions and conflict between those organizations, which we have to respond [to] with that type of communication. There are also . . . times of conflict between those organizations and other organizations.

Latino faculty and staff also serve as ambassadors of comfort for the students. The ability to comfort students was seen as a significant component in establishing an atmosphere of trust, understanding, and acceptance on campus. This was seen as essential in helping students become successful in all educational endeavors.

In comparing and contrasting the administrators' views on the roles of Latino faculty and staff, we observed that they all agreed on the importance of having Latino professionals as a part of the campus community. They all, however, had different views on what their roles should be and how they contribute to the well-being of the institution and the students. While discussing the roles of Latino faculty and staff with students, we noticed that most students felt that the presence of Latino faculty and staff was either of great importance or of little importance. Some students reported that faculty conveyed a sense of comfort, empowerment, ethic of caring, equality, and the importance of communication.

At one private institution, having Latino faculty who were able to speak Spanish or who had previous experience with the Latino culture fostered a connection between students and professors. At two other institutions, students placed great importance on the roles of Latino faculty and staff. The students stated that having Latino faculty and staff had a strong impact on their motivation to succeed in college. It appeared that Latino professors provided students with a genuine sense of caring and that their support helped empower students to achieve their current and future aspirations. One student noted:

> This sense of support was important because you see someone of your own culture teaching classes and if we had more Hispanic/Latino faculty/professors it would help you connect with or relate to someone within your four-to-five year college process. A couple of professors made a big difference, because I see in them what I could be. I see that if they were able to get their Ph.D. and they came out of the same streets and barrios I grew up in, there's no reason why I can't do it. . . . because they made it. It inspires me to do this. I would like to see more Hispanic professors available.

However, for students at a different university, the role of Latino faculty and staff was not important. One student mentioned that she expected Latino faculty and staff to be of critical importance in her college experience; however, she learned that having professors and staff that practice the ethic of caring was of greater importance. For this student, having a caring and genuine relationship with professors seemed to have the greatest impact on her college experience, and the ethic of caring seemed to be more important than the ethnicity of the professor. This student stated, "[There are] not many minority faculty; at first, it bothered me. However, after working with my mentor [who is Caucasian], I realized she really cared about me and being successful." This student did acknowledge that having minority faculty and staff would contribute to a richer college experience for students, because it can diversify the pool of knowledge on campus.

Another student at the same campus also mentioned the importance of equal treatment as an important characteristic of staff and faculty. This student stated, "Professors, faculty, and staff treat everyone here equally. It makes you feel more comfortable to know that there is equal treatment and that they are not going to judge you based on your ethnic background." This student appeared to place a higher importance on being treated equally than on the ethnicity of campus professionals.

Access to Targeted Funding. Administrators highlighted the many benefits of being an HSI. One such benefit is the opportunity to apply for grants and special funding. These grants allow the improvement of existing programs and services and the opportunity to create new ones, not only for Latino students but for the entire campus. One administrator spoke of these benefits to the general campus:

> Funds that are generated by special grants for HSIs are not just for the Latino students. They affect the entire [population] of the institution, so that everybody benefits from these funds. The administration of the college is very happy about that, because it's not just for Latino students, it's everybody.

With the inclusion of all minority-serving institutions in the Higher Education Act of 1965, federal grants and programs are accessible to all underrepresented students on a campus, regardless of the particular minority group served. An administrator discussed this benefit: "[There are] monies out there that you have to write and compete for . . . , but we have been successful at doing that. There are many grants out there . . . that focus in on students that are underrepresented in higher education."

Thus, attending a HSI may be beneficial for all students, not just Latino students. While many programs are directed at underrepresented students, many are accessible to all students, allowing all students to experience the benefits of additional funding and programs that are dependent on HSI status.

The Future of Hispanic-Serving Institutions

The future of HSIs is full of opportunities and challenges. As Latino populations within the United States continue to grow, more Latino students will be entering higher education. This creates a new responsibility for institutions of higher education as they educate Latinos to become future community leaders. As one administrator pointed out:

> [Latino] population growth will also lead to political influence, and it is a group that higher education needs to work carefully and closely with. . . . We want them to be good citizens and contributors. . . . which means we cannot turn our backs on them for education or services.

This administrator's concern stresses the importance of educating what will soon be the largest minority group in the United States. It is imperative that higher education support the development of Latino leaders. Student leadership and empowerment programs specifically targeted at Latino students are needed on today's college campuses.

Diversified Funding Sources. HSIs need to find ways to increase funding for institutions and their students. While the need for monies for HSIs and Latino students is increasing, some administrators noted that available funds have been decreasing in recent years. An administrator in California emphasized this point, saying, "We face serious economic problems in respect to education at all levels." Many Latino students depend on financial aid and low tuition to be able to attend college. For this reason, higher education needs to secure outside funding sources to supplement decreased state support. One possibility could include developing partnerships with engineering- and science-related industries that are in need of educated Latinos. Collaboration between higher education and the private sector could not only increase dollars for programs and scholarships but also create new learning opportunities for students through internship programs.

HSIs must also make efforts to change societal views of Latino students. This includes dispelling misconceptions and stereotypes. According to one administrator, in order for "HSIs to grow, there must be large societal understanding of the [Latino] population and their contribution to society." Another administrator took this idea one step further, stating, "There is a need to look at Hispanic students not as a special need population but as students from a different culture. Administrators need to create environments where everyone has the same opportunities, the same attention." This same administrator also acknowledged the difficulty in making such a change in perceptions: "This would take a cultural change within the institution to realize that there is no such thing as a 'traditional student' anymore." Administrators must be responsive to the changing demographics of their campus. As the notion of a traditional student fades, student service professionals need to create new programs and services that can address the needs of their diverse campus population.

Collaboration with Other Entities. There is also a need for HSIs to collaborate with other entities in order to create a stronger and more unified front to help Latino students. One California administrator suggested that HACU continue to lobby Congress in an effort to increase federal support:

> Our population is growing; it's not getting smaller. What you're getting is larger numbers of the population who have a lot of needs with respect to education and less money given by the state. We need a spokesperson, an advocate, and HACU can be that advocate.

This administrator espoused increased collaboration between HSIs, corporations, and high schools that serve large Latino populations. These entities can work together to meet the overall goal of educating Latino students. For example, through campus visits and mentoring programs, we can bridge the gap between high schools and HSIs. This will help to create a smoother transition for Latino students and provide awareness of higher education on the part of Latino parents. A collaborative effort between HSIs and corporations can provide Hispanic students not only with scholarship dollars but with practical experience and an easier transition to the workforce.

Diversifying Future Educators. At a California institution, an administrator discussed the need to prepare Latino students to become future educators. His ideal is to have more qualified minority teachers in the profession working with students. "Teacher preparation is real critical. [We need to] try to encourage more Latino teachers . . . more folks that come from low-income and first-generation backgrounds." Teachers with similar experiences and backgrounds can encourage more low-income and first-generation students to continue with their education. They can serve as role models for Latino youth, showing them that they too can attain a college degree; this will be a crucial ingredient in achieving the goal of educating Latinos. Latino teachers will understand many of the unique needs of Latinos and the cultural challenges they face; and thus, they will be uniquely equipped to guide Latino students through the educational process.

The Importance of Community. An important element in Latino student success is community. Latino students appear to thrive in environments where there is continual support and concern for their well-being. They need to feel that they matter and are valued members of the campus environment. Tight-knit communities with other Latino students help to create a supportive climate in which students can share similar experiences. Strong relationships with faculty and staff also contribute to a sense of belonging for Latino students. While some students favored having Latino staff and faculty, for other students, it was important only that faculty and staff support them, regardless of race or ethnicity. Higher education should encourage programs that develop a sense of community for Latino students, whether in the residence halls or through support groups, student organizations, or mentoring programs. Future research should investigate the importance of these learning communities or other campus programs and their effectiveness in establishing communities and promoting overall collegiate success for Latino students. Close ties to the community and family are common Latino values, and campuses that can foster this tight-knit community will help to ensure greater success for their Latino student population.

Diversifying Experiences of Latino Students. There is also a need to expand and diversify the experiences of Latino students. Once HSI students leave their institutions, they will be entering an environment that is likely to be highly diverse. HSIs can help Latino students to broaden their horizons in terms of career choices and furthering their education. It is also necessary for HSIs to expose their students to other cultures and experiences in order to create more confidence in these students once they graduate.

It is important to remember that while Latino students are very similar in their backgrounds, there is also a multitude of different countries and cultures within the Latino population. Each student may identify with a different country of origin or cultural heritage. It is essential for HSIs to recognize and celebrate these differences. HSIs must not lose sight of the individual in the process of serving Latino students. In the future, it will be beneficial for HSIs to identify the different subcultures within their Latino student population, as well as recognize the unique perspective and experiences of each individual student.

Conclusion

Overall, it is imperative that the higher education community help educate the general public about the importance of Hispanic-serving institutions. As Latino populations continue to grow and become a central population on the college campus, the number of HSIs will also increase. Institutions will no longer have a choice as to whether to cater to the Latino student population. Therefore, it is to their advantage for colleges and universities to create supportive environments that recognize individual differences.

References

Devarics, C. "House Broadens Hispanic Definition." *Black Issues in Higher Education*, 1998, *15*(7), 6.

Devarics, C. "Budget Increases for HBCUs, HSIs May Fall Short of Goals." *Black Issues in Higher Education*, 2002, *19*(16), 6–8.

Hispanic Association of Colleges and Universities. "Facts on Hispanic Higher Education." 2004. [http://www.hacu.net/hacu/Data,_Statistics,_and_Research1_EN.asp?SnID=118777951]. Retrieved Feb. 3, 2004.

Laden, B. V. "Hispanic-Serving Institutions: Myths and Realities." *Peabody Journal of Education*, 2001, *76*(1), 73–93.

McGoldrick, M., Giordano, J., and Pearce, J. K. *Ethnicity and Family Therapy*. (2nd ed.) New York: Guilford Press, 1996.

O'Brien, E. M., and Zudak, C. "Minority-Serving Institutions: An Overview." In J. P. Merisotis and C. T. O'Brien (eds.), *Minority-Serving Institutions: Distinct Purposes, Common Goals*. New Directions for Higher Education, no. 102. San Francisco: Jossey-Bass, 1998.

Stearns, C., and Watanabe, S. *Hispanic Serving Institutions: Statistical Trends from 1990–1999*. Report No. NCES 2002–051. Washington, D.C.: National Center for Education Statistics, U.S. Department of Education, 2002.

St. John, E. "United We Stand: NAFEO, HACU, and AIHEC Have Formed a New Alliance to Improve Support for Students of Color." *Black Issues in Higher Education*, 1999, *16*, 16–17.

U.S. Department of Education "1998 Amendments to the Higher Education Act of 1965." PL105–244. n.d. [http://ed.gov/policy/highered/leg/hea98/sec501.html]. Retrieved Feb. 2, 2004.

U.S. Department of Education. "Developing Hispanic-Serving Institutions Program." [http://www.ed.gov/programs/idueshsi/index.html]. n.d. Retrieved Mar. 4, 2003.

U.S. Department of Education. "Strengthening Hispanic-Serving Institutions" (Title III, Part A). CFDA No. 84.031. n.d. [http://www.ed.gov/pubs/Biennial/95–96/eval/517–97.pdf]. Retrieved Mar. 4, 2003.

Wolanin, T. R. "The Federal Investment in Minority-Serving Institutions." In J. P. Merisotis and C. T. O'Brien (eds.), *Minority-Serving Institutions: Distinct Purposes, Common Goals*. New Directions for Higher Education, no. 102. San Francisco: Jossey-Bass, 1998.

BOUALOY DAYTON *is a graduate student in the Student Development in Higher Education master's degree program at California State University, Long Beach.*

NANCY GONZALEZ-VASQUEZ *is a graduate student in the Student Development in Higher Education master's degree program at California State University, Long Beach.*

CARLA R. MARTINEZ *is a graduate student in the Student Development in Higher Education master's degree program at California State University, Long Beach.*

CARYN PLUM *is a graduate student in the Student Development in Higher Education master's degree program at California State University, Long Beach.*

4

Critical race theory requires the examination of institutional policies, programs, and practices that interfere with Latino students' rights and abilities to receive the best educational opportunities available within higher education. With attention to an ethic of caring and social justice, student services staff can work to undo the effects of racism on campus.

Practical Considerations of Critical Race Theory and Latino Critical Theory for Latino College Students

Octavio Villalpando

Latinos have rarely been studied in the field of higher education (Olivas, 1986), yet they are the largest and fastest-growing racial or ethnic group (Gandara, 1994), and remain the least-well-educated major population group in the United States (Chapa, 1991). The major challenges facing Latinos with respect to access, persistence, and graduation in higher education have been well documented by Aguirre and Martinez (1993) and by the contributors to this volume. Higher education has attempted to meet the academic and social needs of this increasingly important population by adopting traditional institutional responses, such as providing special college outreach and transition programs, enhancing academic support services, and involving Latino college graduates as mentors and role models.

Despite these institutional efforts, elsewhere in this volume (see Chapters One and Three) data are presented that seriously challenge the extent to which they are yielding a level of success commensurate with the increasing representation of Latinos in higher education. Indeed, when we factor in the current political and institutional retrenchment in providing race-sensitive support programs, we cannot help but wonder how higher education will respond to the increasing needs of Latinos in the future.

In this chapter, I propose the adoption of a unique framework to guide future forms of institutional responses that are quite different from the types of programs and services traditionally adopted to meet the needs of Latino college students. Drawing from critical race theory (CRT) and

Latino critical theory (LatCrit), I suggest various ways by which higher education practitioners can more fully understand and more appropriately respond to the academic and sociocultural needs of Latino college students. The overview that I provide in this chapter is framed within the context of the experiences of Latinos in higher education and includes a discussion of the types of practice and policy implications that could be drawn from CRT and LatCrit to enhance the success of Latinos in college.

Overview of Critical Race Theory and Latino Critical Theory

Critical race theory and Latino critical theory are conceptual frameworks arising from legal studies that can help improve our understanding of issues related to social justice and racial inequality in society (Crenshaw, Gotanda, Peller, and Thomas, 1995; Delgado, 1995; Matsuda, Lawrence, Delgado, and Crenshaw, 1993). These frameworks enable us to analyze patterns of racial exclusion and other forms of discrimination against college students. While legally sanctioned racial discrimination may no longer exist overtly in American higher education, CRT and LatCrit help us recognize patterns, practices, and policies of racial inequality that continue to exist in more insidious and covert ways. CRT and LatCrit can expose these insidious practices and help us dismantle them and remove their obstruction to the success of Latinos in higher education.

Both CRT and LatCrit are being increasingly adopted by education scholars interested in using the K–12 schooling process (Ladson-Billings, 1998; Ladson-Billings and Tate, 1995; Parker, Deyhle, Villenas, and Nebecker, 1998; Solórzano, 1997; Solórzano and Delgado Bernal, 2001; Solórzano and Yosso, 2001; and Tate, 1997), and higher education (Delgado Bernal and Villalpando, 2002; Solórzano and Villalpando, 1998; Solórzano and Delgado Bernal, 2001; Taylor, 1999; Teranishi, 2002; Villalpando, 2003; Villalpando and Delgado Bernal, 2002; and Yosso, 2001) to analyze the racialized barriers erected against people of color. CRT and LatCrit help expose the ways in which so-called race-neutral institutional policies and practices perpetuate racial or ethnic subordination. These frameworks emphasize the importance of viewing practices, policies, and policymaking within a proper historical and cultural context in order to better understand their relationship to race and racism (Crenshaw, Gotanda, Peller, and Thomas, 1995).

While there are many theoretical similarities between CRT and LatCrit, they are distinct in important ways. LatCrit is complementary to CRT (Valdes, 1996), having derived from CRT partly out of a need to address issues that were broader than race/ethnicity in the case of Latinos. Like CRT, LatCrit was conceived as a social justice project (LatCrit Primer, 2000). It encompasses all of the assumptions and underpinnings of CRT but focuses more specifically on the experiences of and realities of Latinos

(Valdes, 1996). LatCrit helps to analyze issues that CRT cannot or does not, like language, immigration, ethnicity, culture, identity, phenotype, and sexuality (Hernandez-Truyol, 1997; Montoya, 1994; Martinez, 1994). LatCrit is a more valid and reliable lens through which to analyze Latinos' multidimensional identities and can address the intersecting issues of racism, sexism, heterosexism, classism, and other forms of oppression of Latinos more appropriately than CRT (Solórzano and Yosso, 2001). Delgado Bernal (2002) observes that LatCrit allows us to look at Latinos' identity at the intersections of immigration, migration, human rights, language, gender, and class (Hernandez-Truyol, 1997).

Following are five defining elements that form the basic assumptions, perspectives, and pedagogies of CRT and LatCrit (Matsuda, Lawrence, Delgado, and Crenshaw, 1993; Solórzano and Delgado Bernal, 2001; Tate, 1997; Villalpando and Delgado Bernal, 2002).

CRT and LatCrit focus on race and racism. CRT and LatCrit acknowledge as their most basic premise that race and racism are a defining characteristic of American society and, by extension, are embedded in the structures, discourses, and policies that guide the daily practices of college campuses (Taylor, 1999). Race and racism are central constructs, but LatCrit proposes that they also intersect with other dimensions of Latinos' identity, such as language, generation status, gender, sexuality, and class (Valdes, 1996). For Latinos, each of these dimensions of their identity can potentially elicit multiple forms of subordination, and each dimension can also be subjected to different forms of oppression. For example, class oppression, racial oppression, and gender oppression do not operate in isolation of one another. It is nearly impossible to identify the specific reason for oppression when an individual may be oppressed for any of these reasons. There is also an exponential effect of these oppressions interacting with one another—the overarching effect is not simply cumulative. In other words, when a Latina student experiences cultural alienation and isolation in college, this experience is not only based on her ethnicity as a Latina but is also influenced by how she is treated as a woman, as a member of a certain socioeconomic class, and in relation to her English language proficiency, her sexual identity, and her perceived immigrant generational status. Thus, while CRT and LatCrit underscore the importance of considering how race and racism affect the experiences of college students of color, LatCrit is especially conscious of accounting for how additional dimensions of identity might also be subjected to additional or different forms of discrimination or marginalization in the case of Latinos (Solórzano and Villalpando, 1998).

CRT and LatCrit analyses suggest that student services practitioners interested in creating truly holistic and more meaningful programs or services for Latinos begin by consciously acknowledging that these students might experience varying degrees and forms of racial discrimination at their university. While it is becoming rarer for students of color to be exposed to overtly hostile acts of racism (such as being verbally harassed with racial epithets), it is not becoming any less rare for them to be subjected to more covert and subtle racial microaggressions (Solórzano, 1998), such as comments made by professors and advisors referencing a student's lack of ability or by campus programming that excludes Latinos. Space limitations do not permit an exhaustive list of examples of these more subtle forms of racism that students and faculty of color must often face, but they have been increasingly well documented in the research literature in higher education (for example, see Smith, 2002; Villalpando, 2003).

Admittedly, it is a rare student services professional who has had any training on how to recognize, let alone take into account, racism in the lives of Latinos or other students of color in higher education. Rather than basing programs or services on uninformed assumptions about what may constitute an approach that accounts for racism, it may be more productive and reliable to simply ask students directly about their needs, either by convening small focus groups or through other systematic methodological approaches. Regardless of the methodological approach, it would also be wise to consult with faculty or others who are knowledgeable about forms of racial discrimination in order to provide an organizing framework for the students' feedback.

CRT and LatCrit contest dominant ideology. CRT and LatCrit challenge the traditional claims of universities to objectivity, meritocracy, color blindness, race neutrality, and equal opportunity. In other words, these theoretical frameworks reveal how the dominant ideology of color blindness and race neutrality acts as a camouflage for the self-interest, power, and privilege of dominant groups in American society (Calmore, 1992; Delgado, 1989).

For example, higher education operates under the illusion that Latinos have an opportunity to succeed that is equal to that of majority white students. CRT and LatCrit challenge this ideology by exposing how, for example, notions of meritocracy and race neutrality in the college admission process benefit majority white students while harming Latinos. For instance, the recent attacks on race-sensitive admissions argue that it is unmeritorious and discriminatory against whites to consider a person's race in determining college admissions. Yet there is an explicit refusal to explain why it is meritorious to continue the allegedly race-neutral practice of factoring in alumni legacy status during the admissions process. The empirical data on college graduation rates show that whites far outnumber Latinos as college alumni; thus the legacy factor in college admissions clearly favors whites over Latinos and other groups of color.however, higher education institutions appear to insist that this is a meritocratic and race-neutral admissions practice. CRT and LatCrit can help practitioners question in regard to false notions of racial objectivity and equal opportunity in the dominant ideology that guides everyday practices in higher education.

The often unacknowledged dominant ideologies of color-blind fairness and race-neutral meritocracy on which higher education bases much of its student support services must be challenged by practitioners who are truly committed to creating holistic programs and services for Latinos. CRT and LatCrit provide the lens through which student services professionals can contest the premises that inform the development of programs, policies, and practices designed to enhance the educational experiences of Latinos. For example, a LatCrit lens suggests that it is not reverse discrimination to advocate for the creation of a program designed specifically for Latino college students. Rather, such a program constitutes a requisite acknowledgment of the institution's historical legacy of exclusion (Hurtado, Milem, Clayton-Pedersen, and Allen, 1998) and a culturally relevant response that attempts to understand the importance of Latinos' identity in their success. LatCrit requires higher education to acknowledge that the dominant ideologies of alleged color blindness in practice only serve to benefit majority white students while further disadvantaging Latinos and other students of color.

CRT and LatCrit focus on social justice and social justice practice. CRT and LatCrit have a fundamental commitment to work toward achieving social justice. These frameworks consider social justice to be a legitimate struggle to eliminate all forms of subordination on the basis of race, gender, language, generation status, sexual preference, and class (Matsuda, 1996). This is an especially relevant CRT and LatCrit tenet for higher education practitioners who already often share a deep commitment to an ethic of caring (Noddings, 1984) and service.

At its core, the application of this tenet suggests that it is appropriate and, indeed, expected that institutions and individuals strive toward achieving educational equality for all students. This ought to be one of the easiest CRT and LatCrit tenets to facilitate by student services personnel given the altruistic value-orientation of their profession. This tenet of social justice gives student services permission to actualize their profession's aspirations to an ethic of caring and service by rooting those aspirations in a social justice agenda.

It is important to understand how a focus on practice based in social justice moves beyond the well-meaning holistic approach that emphasizes the education of the whole student (intellectual, emotional, and social development), an approach that student services professionals adopt in their everyday practice. A CRT and LatCrit focus on social justice practice allows student services professionals to openly acknowledge that the influence and motivation for their work is based on a desire to eliminate all forms of subordination in higher education. In other words, a LatCrit social justice practice enables a director of campus activities to develop programs, services, and practices that are explicitly designed to target, for example, the elimination of racist or heterosexist stereotypes about gay or lesbian Latinos that often exist in the Greek system. While the motivation and goals for this example of programming could likely fit both a holistic student development and a social justice–based approach, a LatCrit framework would enable the campus activities director to be much more explicit about the social justice purpose behind her or his efforts.

Coincidentally, student services professionals would likely find willing allies and partners in the implementation of this CRT/LatCrit tenet among Latino students and other students of color, who often come to college with a strong commitment to achieving social justice for their communities (Delgado Bernal, 2002; Villalpando, 1996, 2003).

CRT and LatCrit recognize experiential knowledge. CRT and LatCrit recognize that the experiential knowledge of people of color is legitimate and critical to understanding racial inequality. For Latinos, the application of a CRT and LatCrit framework requires that their experiential knowledge be central and viewed as a resource stemming directly from their lived experiences. Within this tenet, their experiential knowledge is viewed as an asset, a form of community memory, a source of empowerment and strength, and not as a deficit. This tenet requires higher education practitioners to actively integrate the experiential knowledge of Latino college students into the process of conceptualizing and implementing more responsive and culturally relevant programs and services. Support services that build on the experiential knowledge of Latino college students ensure that they reflect an understanding that these students have often experienced varying levels of racism, discrimination, and other forms of oppression, instead of assuming that these experiences do not exist or are unimportant to their academic success. Support services and their providers must also recognize the agency, vitality, and strength that Latino college students have demonstrated just to get to college, let alone to persist, excel, and graduate from an alienating educational system.

Students' experiential knowledge can come from various sources and be demonstrated through different means, but often the best way to recognize this knowledge is by simply asking the students about their experiences before and at college. By doing so, one would learn that their experiential knowledge is often passed on to them by their family through storytelling, family histories, biographies, scenarios, parables, *cuentos* (stories), chronicles, and narratives (Delgado, 1989, 1995; Olivas, 1986).

At its most basic level, this tenet requires that Latinos not be viewed as deficient or disadvantaged because of their racial or ethnic identity, gender, class, immigration status, generation status, or language ability. If Latinos are disadvantaged in any way, it is as a result of not having access to better-resourced schools, a competent health care system, or fair-paying jobs. Indeed, it is not their culture or race but the educational system that has placed them at the greatest disadvantage, and as college students, they have to contend with a system that assumes that they and their culture are to blame for their lack of success. The CRT-LatCrit tenet of valuing experiential knowledge underscores the need to understand how their identities as Latinos can actually nourish and empower their personal and academic success in college.

CRT and LatCrit focus on historical context. CRT and LatCrit challenge ahistoricism in higher education research, policy, and practice. This tenet insists that policies and practices in higher education be viewed through a historical lens in order to understand how they will affect Latinos and other students of color (Delgado, 1984, 1992; Hurtado, Milem, Clayton-Pedersen, and Allen, 1998; Olivas, 1986). For example, it is important to understand how their history, which involves educational tracking and substandard schools, has affected Latinos' entry into higher education. Rather than accept the prevailing myths that Latinos and other students of color come from families that do not value higher education, this CRT and LatCrit tenet insists that we recognize how they have traditionally been tracked by ineffective schools into non-college-bound majors, which has resulted in their disproportionate attendance at community colleges that frequently decreases aspirations rather than sustains or builds them, a process termed "cooling out" by Burton Clark (1980). In order to develop culturally relevant services and programs for Latinos, CRT and LatCrit call for a deeper understanding of the historical factors that have affected and continue to affect their lives and educational experiences.

This tenet requires student services professionals to acquire a better understanding of the historical and current experiences of the communities from which Latino students come. It is important to understand, for example, whether Latino students may be coming from regional or local farm-working families who are likely to have a vastly different economic experience from middle-class Latinos. Likewise, farm-working families are likely to have a different history and experience in the United States from middle-class Latinos. These are the types of important differences that may surface in a historical analysis of the origins and precollege experiences of Latino students. Equally important is understanding how to take account of these origins and experiences in the development of services and programs that are designed to serve Latinos. The growing heterogeneity of Latinos in higher education requires that student services professionals not adopt a one-size-fits-all approach to programming but remain conscious of historical and regional differences within the group. Indeed, perhaps the only constant within the heterogeneous population of Latinos may be having experienced the effects of racism.

Conclusion

These defining elements of CRT and LatCrit form a framework that has applications in how we serve Latino college students. CRT and LatCrit are especially helpful in improving our understanding of the experiences of Latinos in higher education, given how U.S. society has historically used race, ethnicity, national origin, language, class, and an ever-changing conception of justice in the construction and implementation of laws that influence higher education (Solórzano and Yosso, 2000; Taylor, 1999). These theoretical frameworks help us examine the relationship between race and racism in the structures, processes, and discourses within higher education by, for example, pointing to the contradictory ways in which universities operate, with their potential to oppress and marginalize as well as emancipate and empower students (Solórzano and Villalpando, 1998).

Even as American higher education experiences and anticipates ever-growing enrollments of Latinos, opportunistic political forces are compelling institutions to dismantle race-sensitive support services and programs designed to improve the educational experiences and outcomes of this student population. As Latino enrollments have increased, we have not seen a proportional increase in their rates of success (Solorzano and Villalpando, 1998), and clearly, given the current erosion of race-sensitive outreach and support services, the prospects for improving their success in the future are not encouraging.

Critical race theory and Latino critical theory offer unique approaches to understanding and meeting the needs of Latinos in higher education. Indeed, these frameworks offer an opportunity to reverse the trend of declining quantity and quality of services for this growing student population. By focusing attention on alleged race-neutral and color-blind practices that in actuality are clearly quite racially biased and exclusionary, CRT and LatCrit can help higher education practitioners develop more responsive and comprehensive approaches that enhance the educational experiences of Latino college students. These frameworks offer a way to analyze current practices in colleges and universities and to develop more culturally relevant practices that integrate Latinos' sociohistorical and cultural knowledge and experiences. CRT and LatCrit attempt to account for the contradictions and inconsistencies that have guided and continue to guide the development of policies and practices that affect educational equality for Latino college students. When student services professionals use CRT and LatCrit to carefully assess their policies, practices, and programs for inequality, contradictions, and inconsistencies, they can increase college satisfaction and success rates of all students who experience oppression in the collegiate environment.

References

Aguirre, A., and Martinez, R. *Chicanos in Higher Education: Issues and Dilemmas for the 21st Century.* ASHE-ERIC Higher Education Report No. 3. Washington, D.C.: School of Education and Human Development, George Washington University, 1993.

Calmore, J. "Critical Race Theory, Archie Shepp, and Fire Music: Securing an Authentic Intellectual Life in a Multicultural World." *Southern California Law Review,* 1992, *65,* 2129–2231.

Chapa, J. "Special Focus: Hispanic Demographic and Educational Trends." In D. J. Carter and R. Wilson (eds.), *Minorities in Higher Education.* Ninth Annual Status Report. Washington, D.C.: American Council on Education, 1991.

Clark, B. R. "The 'Cooling Out' Function Revisited." In G. B. Vaughan (ed.), *Questioning the Community College Role.* New Directions for Community Colleges, no. 32. San Francisco: Jossey-Bass, 1980.

Crenshaw, K., Gotanda, N., Peller, G., and Thomas, K. *Critical Race Theory: The Key Writings That Formed the Movement.* New York: New Press, 1995.

Delgado, R. "The Imperial Scholar: Reflections on a Review of Civil Rights Literature." *University of Pennsylvania Law Review,* 1984, *132,* 561–578.

Delgado, R. "Storytelling for Oppositionists and Others: A Plea for Narrative." *Michigan Law Review,* 1989, 87, 2411–2441.

Delgado, R. "Rodrigo's Chronicle." *Yale Law Review,* 1992, *101,* 1357–1383.

Delgado, R. *The Rodrigo Chronicles: Conversations about America and Race.* New York: New York University Press, 1995.

Delgado Bernal, D. "Critical Race Theory, Latino Critical Theory, and Critical Raced-Gendered Epistemologies: Recognizing Students of Color as Holders and Creators of Knowledge." *Qualitative Inquiry,* 2002, *8*(1), 105–126.

Delgado Bernal, D., and Villalpando, O. "The Apartheid of Knowledge in the Academy: The Struggle over 'Legitimate'" Knowledge for Faculty of Color." *Journal of Equity and Excellence in Education,* 2002, *35*(2). (Special Issue on Critical Race Theory in Education).

Gandara, P. "Choosing Higher Education: Educationally Ambitious Chicanos and the Path to Social Mobility." *Education Policy Analysis Archives,* 1994, *2*(8).

Hernandez-Truyol, B. E. "Borders (En)gendered: Normativities, Latinas, and a LatCrit Paradigm." *New York University Law Review,* 1997, 72, 882.

Hurtado, S., Milem, J. F., Clayton-Pedersen, A. R., and Allen, W. R. *Enacting Diverse Learning Environments: Improving the Climate for Racial/Ethnic Diversity in Higher Education.* ASHE-ERIC Higher Education Report, Vol. 26, No. 8. Washington, D.C.: Graduate School of Education and Human Development, George Washington University, 1998.

Ladson-Billings, G. "Just What Is Critical Race Theory and What's It Doing in a Nice Field Like Education?" In L. Parker, D. Deyhle, S. Villenas, and K. Nebecker (eds.), *Critical Race Theory and Qualitative Research in Education.* (Special issue). *International Journal of Qualitative Studies in Education,* 1998, *11*(1).

Ladson-Billings, G., and Tate, W. "Toward a Critical Race Theory of Education." *Teachers College Record,* 1995, *97,* 47–68.

LatCrit Primer. "Fact Sheet: LatCrit." Presentation to the 5th Annual LatCrit Conference, "Class in LatCrit: Theory and Praxis in the World of Economic Inequality," Breckenridge, Colo., May 4–7, 2000.

Martinez, G. A. "Legal Interdeterminacy, Judicial Discretion, and the Mexican-American Litigation Experience: 1930–1980." *UC Davis Law Review,* 1994, *27,* 555–618.

Matsuda, M. *Where Is Your Body? Essays on Race, Gender and the Law.* Boston: Beacon Press, 1996.

Matsuda, M., Lawrence, C., Delgado, R., and Crenshaw, K. (eds.). *Words That Wound: Critical Race Theory, Assaultive Speech, and the First Amendment.* Boulder, Colo.: Westview Press, 1993.

Montoya, M. "Mascaras, Trenzas, y Grenas: Un/masking the Self While Un/Braiding Latina Stories and Legal Discourse." *Chicano/Latino Law Review* (UCLA School of Law), 1994, *15*(1), 1–37.

Noddings, N. *Caring, A Feminine Approach to Ethics and Moral Education.* Berkeley: University of California Press, 1984.

Olivas, M. (ed.). *Latino College Students.* New York: Teachers College Press, 1986.

Parker, L., Deyhle, D., Villenas, S., and Nebecker, K. (eds.). *Critical Race Theory and Qualitative Research in Education.* (Special issue). *International Journal of Qualitative Studies in Education,* 1998, *11*(1).

Smith, W. A. "Black Faculty Coping with Racial Battle Fatigue: The Campus Racial

Climate in a Post-Civil Rights Era." In D. Cleveland (ed.), *Broken Silence: Conversations About Race by African Americans at Predominantly White Institutions.* New York: Peter Lang, 2002.

Solórzano, D. G. "Images and Words That Wound: Critical Race Theory, Racial Stereotyping and Teacher Education." *Teacher Education Quarterly,* 1997, *24,* 5–19.

Solórzano, D. G. "Critical Race Theory, Racial and Gender Microaggressions, and the Experiences of Chicana and Chicano Scholars." *International Journal of Qualitative Studies in Education,* 1998, *11,* 121–136.

Solórzano, D. G., and Delgado Bernal, D. "Examining Transformational Resistance Through a Critical Race and LatCrit Theory Framework: Chicana and Chicano Students in an Urban Context." *Urban Education,* 2001, *36*(3), 308–342.

Solórzano, D. G., and Villalpando, O. "Critical Race Theory, Marginality, and the Experiences of Students of Color in Higher Education." In C. A. Torres and T. A. Mitchell (eds.), *Sociology of Education: Emerging Perspectives.* New York: State University of New York Press, 1998.

Solórzano, D. G., and Yosso, T. "Toward a Critical Race Theory of Chicana and Chicano Education." In C. Tejeda, C. Martinez, and Z. Leonardo (eds.), *Charting New Terrains of Chicana(o)/Latina(o) Education.* Cresskill, N.J.: Hampton Press, 2000.

Solórzano, D. G., and Yosso, T. "Critical Race and LatCrit Theory and Method: Counter-Storytelling, Chicana and Chicano Graduate School Experiences." *International Journal of Qualitative Studies in Education,* 2001, *14*(4), 471–495.

Tate, W. "Critical Race Theory and Education: History, Theory, and Implications." *Review of Research in Education,* 1997, *22,* 195–247.

Taylor, E. "Critical Race Theory and Interest Convergence in the Desegregation of Higher Education." In L. Parker, D. Deyhle, and S. Villenas (eds.), *Race Is. . . . Race Isn't: Critical Race Theory and Qualitative Studies in Education.* Boulder, Colo.: Westview Press, 1999.

Teranishi, R. "Asian Pacific Americans and Critical Race Theory: An Examination of School Racial Climate." *Journal of Equity and Excellence in Education,* 2002, *35*(2). (Special Issue on Critical Race Theory in Education).

Valdes, F. "Latina/o Ethnicities, Critical Race Theory, and Post-Identity Politics in Postmodern Legal Culture: From Practices to Possibilities." *La Raza Law Journal,* Spring 1996, *9*(1).

Villalpando, O. "The Long-Term Effects of College on Chicana and Chicano College Students' 'Other-Oriented' Values, Service Careers, and Community Involvement." Unpublished doctoral dissertation, University of California, Los Angeles, 1996.

Villalpando, O. "Self Segregation or Self Preservation? A Critical Race Theory and Latina/o Critical Theory Analysis of a Study of Chicana/o Students." *International Journal of Qualitative Studies in Education,* 2003, *16*(5).

Villalpando, O., and Delgado Bernal, D. "A Critical Race Theory Analysis of Barriers That Impede the Success of Faculty of Color." In W. Smith, P. Altbach, and K. Lomotey (eds.), *The Racial Crisis in American Higher Education.* (2nd ed.) New York: State University of New York Press, 2002.

Yosso, T. J. "Critical Race, LatCrit Theory, and Critical Media Literacy: Chicana/o Students' Resilient Resistance to Visual Microaggressions." Unpublished doctoral dissertation, University of California, Los Angeles, 2001.

OCTAVIO VILLALPANDO *is assistant professor of educational leadership and policy and director of the Center for the Study of Race and Diversity in Higher Education at the University of Utah.*

5

Community colleges serve as the point of entry for the majority of Latinos in higher education, offering low-cost, smaller-scale educational opportunities in the communities where students live and providing the preparation for four-year colleges and universities that may have been lacking in their K–12 education. The challenges to community colleges in providing services to Latinos are great, but their potential to facilitate the achievement of Latinos is vast.

Latinos at Community Colleges

Magadelena Martinez, Edith Fernández

As former community college administrators, we approached the creation of this chapter by asking what types of information would have been helpful as we interacted with Latino students, faculty, and other administrators on a daily basis and attempted to facilitate student learning, adaptation, and academic success. Knowing that institutional needs and priorities vary depending on a number of internal and external variables, we offer an introduction to some of the most salient issues that affect Latino students attending community colleges as well as community colleges' ability to facilitate Latino student success.

Community colleges absorb a significant percentage of first-time college students. Two-year community colleges make up close to 50 percent of all colleges and universities, and their collective enrollment constitutes over 70 percent of all undergraduate students in higher education. Minority students represent 21 percent of all students enrolled in higher education, yet they constitute over 60 percent of the total enrollment in community colleges (*Chronicle of Higher Education,* 2002). (For the purposes of this discussion, the term *minority* refers to students who are African American, Latino, or Native American.) Low tuition, proximity to home, availability of evening courses, flexible schedules, remedial education, and open admissions are characteristics of community colleges that help to explain this phenomenal growth.

Latino Participation in Community Colleges

For Latinos, community colleges often represent a stepping-stone to a bachelor's degree. Latino students are far more likely to be enrolled in two-year colleges than students from any other racial or ethnic group. Latinos

NEW DIRECTIONS FOR STUDENT SERVICES, no. 105, Spring 2004 © Wiley Periodicals, Inc.

represent 9 percent of all undergraduate students enrolled in higher education, yet close to 60 percent of Latino college enrollment is in two-year colleges (*Chronicle of Higher Education*, 2002). Within the Latino population, there are significant differences. For instance, Latinos of Mexican origin have the highest proportion of Latinos attending community colleges; almost half of Mexican American students attend two-year colleges (Fry, 2002). This has meaningful societal implications, because Latinos of Mexican descent represent close to 60 percent of the entire U.S. Latino population, and in several major cities, they represent a significant proportion of the population. States where there are significant numbers of Latinos depend on the educational preparedness of Latinos for economic and social stability. For these reasons, the overrepresentation of Latino students in community colleges has triggered a demand for research on the status of Latinos in community colleges, as well as the practices and policies that affect them. The purpose of this chapter is to provide a brief overview of the ways in which community colleges help Latino students achieve their educational and occupational goals, including strategies and programs that integrate family, community, and K–12 school systems.

Educational Aspirations of Latino Students at Community Colleges

For Latinos, community colleges occupy a unique position in higher education as sites for mining the social and cultural capital needed for upward social and economic mobility in the United States. When asked about their educational and occupational goals, Latino students overwhelmingly state at least a bachelor's degree as their intended goal. Research confirms that 50 to 87 percent of Latino students enrolled in community colleges aspire to transfer to a senior institution and complete a baccalaureate degree (Bensimon and Riley, 1984; Rendón, Justiz, and Resta, 1988). These studies point to the desire and motivation of Latinos to achieve higher academic goals that will eventually translate into occupational and career opportunities. Yet institutional, regional, and national studies point to the abysmally low percentage of Latino transfer rates to four-year institutions (Castaneda, 2002; Nora, 1993; Rendón, Justiz, and Resta, 1988; Rendón and Nora, 1989, 1994; Rendón and Valadez, 1993; Suarez, 2003). Studies show how Latinos' attendance at community colleges may adversely affect their chances of transferring, persistence, or completion of any type of degree (Brint and Karabel, 1989; Cohen and Brawer, 1996; Fry, 2002). Recent U.S. Department of Education statistics illuminate how Latino students are more likely to drop out if they begin their college studies at a two-year college (National Center for Education Statistics, 2000). Other studies show attrition rates for Latino students in community colleges as high as 80 percent (Rendón and Nora, 1989). Some suggest that high attrition rates are strongly correlated with students' socioeconomic and academic levels (Cohen and Brawer,

1996; Tinto, 1987). Yet studies show that even after controlling for background, ability, and aspirations, students at community colleges are 10 to 18 percent more likely to drop out of college during the first two years than students at four-year colleges with similar backgrounds (Dougherty, 1992).

Latinos also lag in degree completion rates. Kane and Rouse (1995) found that half of the students who initially enrolled at two-year colleges never completed a postsecondary degree compared with the percentage of students who enroll in a four-year college as first-year students (cited in Fry, 2002). Although some suggest that the mission of community colleges is not exclusively to facilitate the graduation of all students, because many attend for professional development or vocational training, recent trends indicate that a large majority of students—in particular Latino students—who attend community colleges aspire to eventually transfer to a senior institution. Community colleges must critically evaluate their role and examine why so few Latino students successfully navigate through their institutions to achieve their educational goals.

The Community College Transfer Function

Over the last twenty-five years, the transfer function of community colleges has declined significantly (Brint and Karabel, 1989; Cohen and Brawer, 1996; Rendón and Nora, 1994). Today, estimates of students who transfer to senior institutions range from 5 to 15 percent (Rendón and Nora, 1994). Brint and Karabel (1989) suggest that the increase in vocationalism not only marked a decline in the community college transfer function but also accentuated the stratification of higher education, relegating community colleges to the bottom of the hierarchy. The shift to a focus on vocational training has serious implications for how community colleges serve Latino students who enter two-year institutions with the expectation of transferring. Rendón (1999b) suggests that there is a disconnect between the expectations of Latino students and community college policy. Latino students attend community colleges as a gateway to senior institutions, expecting to complete transferable courses and receive the guidance and mentoring necessary to successfully navigate postsecondary institutions. Community college policy, on the other hand, primarily provides resources and support services for students interested in vocational programs, shortchanging the type of curriculum and student services needed to successfully transfer to senior institutions. Rendón (1999b) contends that the problem is not that Latino students lack ambition or ability to work; rather, they have not received the socialization, encouragement, and mentoring to be able to take advantage of higher education. To complicate matters, the lack of systematic study of transfer students and the many ways in which community colleges define a transfer student leave a gap in our understanding of how well community colleges prepare students for transfer.

Nettles and Millett (1999) suggest that a common definition of what constitutes a transfer is needed across all community colleges in order to develop normative standards for institutions to use in monitoring their status and progress. They found that some colleges count as transfers only those students who receive an associate degree, while others include people who have completed a specified number of credit hours, and still others include anyone who ever attended. There have been efforts to devise a common definition of the transfer process. During the period from 1989 to 1993, the National Transfer Center grant program targeted community colleges with significant enrollments of low-income, black, and Latino students to implement an academic model for transfer purposes (Rendón and Nora, 1994). One of the concerns that surfaced was the need for effective measures to determine the success of transfer efforts. With the participation of the Center for the Study of Community Colleges (CSCC), the National Transfer Center program defined the transfer population as "those students who were first-time college attendees who enrolled in community college and earned, in a four-year period, at least twelve college-level credits and then enrolled in a four-year institution" (Rendón and Nora, 1994, p. 147). Those involved with the project suggested that "the transfer definition enables institutions to set transfer goals, include transfer in their strategic planning, and document student flow to determine how many students are benefiting from transfer efforts, what 'works' in transfer, and whether additional institutional efforts are needed" (Rendón and Nora, 1994, p. 149). It is unclear, however, whether this definition was adopted beyond the 164 community colleges that CSCC worked with during the program. Despite this limitation, several transfer studies illuminate the current status of Latinos and suggest some new directions for community colleges.

A comprehensive study that examined the transfer function at community colleges with high Latino student enrollments identified a number of barriers that deterred the transfer process (Rendón, Justiz, and Resta, 1988). Student-centered barriers included a lack of motivation and academic preparation; unfamiliarity with the costs and benefits of the higher education system; unwillingness to leave community and family; lack of family involvement in education; the necessity of having to work to help the family survive; not knowing they were capable of earning a degree; and failure to understand the consequences of changing programs and financial pressures. Institutional barriers included faculty resistance to advising students and low expectations for student academic achievement; lack of clear articulation agreements with senior institutions; and weak efforts to ease student academic and social integration (Rendón and Nora, 1994, p. 124).

A subsequent qualitative study (Suarez, 2003) identified factors that contributed to the transfer of Latino students from a California community college to a four-year state university. Suarez found that students' personal experiences, family struggles, and financial hardships often served as catalysts, motivating students to pursue their bachelor's degree. This "anything is possible" belief is likened to the "culture of possibility" found among high-achieving Chicanos and Chicanas who had graduated from selective institutions (Gandara, 1995). Suarez (2003) suggests that this finding underscores the importance of understanding students' background and the critical role it plays in shaping their educational decisions, actions, and resilience.

Another significant finding in Suarez's study (Suarez, 2003) was the importance of institutional commitment to the transfer function, which was largely mediated through strong external collaborations with senior institutions. These external relationships addressed only part of the puzzle; essential to Latino transfer success was also a sense of shared responsibility among students, faculty, and administrators, although Suarez suggests that faculty participation was minimal and was being showcased rather than faculty being full partners intimately involved in the planning and implementation of the transfer process. Numerous other studies have emphasized the importance of faculty-student interactions, in particular the potential positive or negative results such interactions have on the success of Latino students (Astin, 1982, 1993; Hurtado, Milem, Clayton-Pedersen, and Allen, 1998a, 1998b; Kuh, 1995). To date, the majority of transfer studies have focused on students' actions and behaviors, the utility of college transfer programs, faculty-student interactions, or faculty mentoring and advising. Missing from many of these studies is an examination of how cultural contexts are enacted and how they mediate institutional missions; also missing is an analysis of the roles that faculty, administrators, and students take on.

Rhoads's qualitative approach to organizational analysis examines the politics of culture and identity as revealed through the kinds of discourse and pedagogical strategies enacted at a community college with a high Latino student enrollment (Rhoads, 1999). To situate his analysis, he uses monoculturalism and multiculturalism as categories derived from his theoretical assumptions about culture, identity, and social structures. Monoculturalism is the belief that a singular culture prevails or ought to prevail within a society or organization. Education and pedagogical practices reinforce an authoritarian view, and students are viewed as static participants in the educational process. Multiculturalism is the belief that multiple cultural identities exist within a society and that it is the responsibility of the college to reflect the "different ways of knowing and cultural forms diverse peoples bring to educational institutions" (Rhoads, 1999, p. 115). When this perspective is used, diverse voices are included within the curriculum and within the organizing structures of the institutions. In his analysis, Rhoads found that the majority of faculty, administrators, and staff enacted a monocultural approach, while a small group enacted a multicultural approach to their roles within the community college. Faculty who enacted a multicultural perspective tended to encourage Mexican American students to see their education not only as a vehicle for economic progress but also as a tool for liberation; in other words, the cultivation of critical skills "not just to inform but to transform" their lives (Bensimon, 1994). Community college transfer programs that enacted the ideals of multiculturalism made positive contributions to increasing the transfer rates of participating students: in the program that Rhoads studied, the transfer rate for students was 13.5 percent compared with 9 percent for the overall student population at that college. The program focused on building collaborative relationships between English teachers and Mexican American counselors in order to provide a culturally based academic counseling program for students. Those that viewed their roles from a monocultural standpoint grounded their behaviors in assimilationist perspectives that forced diverse individuals to leave their cultural heritage behind in order to succeed. Rhoads (1999) suggests that many institutions have adopted a monocultural view and succinctly summarizes conditions at the majority of community colleges:

> The challenge facing community colleges . . . is helping faculty, staff, and students to recognize the interconnections between educational processes and student identities. Central to this challenge is coming to terms with the interconnectedness of culture, knowledge, and power. We need to recognize that teaching and learning is a contextualized process in which certain cultural forms become legitimized through their inclusion or delegitimized through their absence. This legitimization process has serious consequences for a student's sense of self and sense of cultural identity. Nowhere perhaps are these issues more relevant than in the context of the community college where more and more diverse students are seeking educational opportunities and social mobility. [p. 121]

If this study is any indication of the direction in which community colleges—in particular those with high minority enrollments—should go, then institutions need to pay closer attention to their cultural contexts and find sites where collaborative relationships can be developed, sustained, and replicated.

Creating Relationship-Centered Community Colleges

Community colleges have been criticized for failing to acknowledge or adapt to the diversity in their student populations, resulting in stubbornly low transfer rates and consistently high dropout rates (Shaw, Rhoads, and Valadez, 1999). It is essential that action steps at the institutional level focus on creating in-class and out-of-class learning environments that validate the academic abilities and efforts of diverse students. Espousing such validation places the onus on college faculty, counselors, and administrative staff to take a proactive role in reaching out to students to affirm them as capable of doing academic work and to support them in their academic endeavors and social adjustment (Rendón, 1999a). High attrition rates and low transfer rates indicate that community colleges must reevaluate their purpose and mission within the broader society. There is no disputing that more can and should be done to help facilitate Latino students realize their educational aspirations. Rendón (1999a) suggests, "community colleges must find ways to enter into relationships with entities concerned with the common work of educating diverse students and strengthening their communities" (p. 1). If community colleges are to change the way they do business and facilitate student success, they must become relationship-centered institutions that focus on internal and external collaboration with all stakeholders. External collaboration focuses on faculty and administrators preserving access and opportunity, helping to minimize K–12 barriers, and preparing students for baccalaureate degrees. Many community colleges have focused on developing relationship-centered initiatives that can serve as models for other institutions interested in creating more inclusive colleges. Rendón (1999a) also puts forth the following recommendations for community colleges interested in creating relationship-centered institutions:

- Community college leaders, faculty, and staff should engage in collaborative analysis and planning to design collaborative community colleges based on the principles of multiculturalism and democracy.
- Community colleges should design validating teaching and learning environments that are relationship-centered, connecting faculty and students.
- Relationship-centered models that engage two-year colleges with feeder K–12 schools should be created in order to design institutional outreach strategies (for example, early intervention, summer bridge programs, and mentoring programs) that target students in the early grades. These models should focus on eradicating access barriers, instilling the idea that college is a viable option, and ensuring that certain requirements are fulfilled in order to attend college.
- Relationship-centered models that involve community colleges learning more about the educational needs of their diverse student clientele should be developed and sustained in order to design instructional programs for students when and where they need them.
- Community colleges should work with local schools and business and industry to design models (school-to-work, youth apprenticeship, tech prep, career academies, and cooperative education) that prepare students to enter the workforce.
- Community colleges should enter into collaborative partnerships with four-year institutions to facilitate the transfer process, establish articulation agreements, initiate Transfer Year Experience Programs at the four-year institutions, and ensure that students are able to attain bachelor's degrees and be poised to enroll in graduate and professional schools.

Programs That Support Latino Students in Achieving Their Educational Goals

This section identifies community college programs that have adapted multicultural ideals that integrate family, community, and K-12 school systems; these programs can serve as models for institutions interested in creating relationship-centered collaborations.

Puente Program, University of California. The Puente Program is perhaps one of the most successful community college programs for Latino students. Initiated in 1981 as a Latino-specific program at Chabot College in Hayward, California, it is now in place in some fifty-five two-year colleges and thirty-six high schools in California. The goals of the program are high school retention and college preparation. Key components include intensive writing instruction, a focus on Latino literature, academic counseling and mentoring, and workshops that integrate family members. The program is premised on the belief that validation of students' life experiences is essential for academic success. Puente's validating teams of instructors, counselors, and mentors play an important role in promoting college access. A validation team provides students with information about what it takes to transfer and earn a degree from a four-year institution, an education plan, solid academic preparation, and knowledge about the socioeconomic payoffs of obtaining a higher education. This is a comprehensive undertaking that links the community to the community college and four-year institutions. A study of the Puente programs indicates that 81 to 90 percent of the 1994–95 entering cohort were still in school and in the program two years later. These retention rates are significantly higher than rates for those who did not participate in the program (Gandara, 1996).

Achieving a College Education (ACE) Program, Maricopa Community Colleges, Arizona. ACE is a collaborative 2+2+2 (two years in high school, two years of community college, two years at a four-year college) program that was originally established in 1987. Its purpose is to increase the number of minority, economically disadvantaged, and at-risk students who attain baccalaureate degrees after successfully completing high school and associate degrees. ACE has successfully collaborated with high schools in two districts and with Arizona State University (ASU) to increase retention and graduation rates. ASU, in conjunction with South Mountain Community College, offers a transfer bridge program for students during their third or fourth summer in the program. The program provides enrollment in a university-level course and a seminar that provides transfer information and a university orientation, a one-week residence hall experience, and orientation for ACE parents (Rendón, 1999a).

Summer Scholars Transfer Institute (SSTI), Santa Ana College, California. SSTI is a joint project involving Santa Ana College, the Los Angeles Community College District, and the University of California at Irvine (UCI). The program serves 150 community college students each summer. SSTI is an eleven-day residential program in which students earn three hours of college credit in one of five courses. Students and faculty meet one month prior to the start of the institute. Students complete extensive reading assignments, participate in classroom activities that stress collaborative learning, and participate in evening study groups. UCI also arranges a transfer day when students meet individually with admissions staff to review their transcripts and discuss admissions requirements. About 95 percent of all students successfully complete the course. Through this program, Santa Ana College has doubled the number of underrepresented students transferring to the University of California. Statewide, Santa Ana College has improved its ranking from forty-fourth to ninth place in number of Chicano/Latino students transferring to the University of California (Rendón, 1999a).

Access to higher education can no longer be narrowly defined in terms of college enrollment. Community colleges must understand that retention, adaptation, and transfer are equally important access issues. Once students enroll in community colleges, they need access to progressive and sustained assistance to ensure that they stay enrolled and graduate from college. The three programs that we just described illustrate how community colleges can address the systemic problems that many Latino students face in higher education. Not only do these programs address practical issues associated with retention and transfer, but they also incorporate and build important connections between faculty, high schools, transfer universities, and Latinos' homes and communities. These programs point to the importance of going beyond intellectual development and attending to the social and personal development of community college students. Validation should be intentional, proactive, and systematic for community college students. There is a high need to build multiple forms of connections to create and sustain much-needed relationship-centered community colleges.

Conclusion

Latinos attend community colleges at a far greater rate than any other ethnic or racial minority. Community colleges have become the dominant educational vehicle of Latinos in pursuit of their dreams through higher education. Therefore, it is essential that we support Latinos from as early as possible in their higher education career. Simply put, policymakers and educational leaders must develop policies aimed at improving educational opportunities at all levels. Policies must support programs that attend to the cultural norms of the community and the political contexts of those communities in order to increase students' access to, enrollment in, and graduation from college. A cookie-cutter approach comprised of solely technical components is not enough.

Community colleges need to move from monoculturalism to multiculturalism. Community colleges must understand the students they serve, who are often low-income, working-class, academically underprepared, first-generation students, and, in most cases, ethnic or racial minorities. These populations of college students are a sharp contrast to those who attend four-year institutions and whose parents have attended college. Students' cultural beliefs and norms must be integrated into program curricula, teaching strategies, and educational resources. Early studies indicate that the enactment of multicultural initiatives has positive results on students' perceptions of their ability and academic attainment.

Establish completion and transfer standards and develop a culture that facilitates achievement of these standards. Currently, there are no national standards for community college completion. However, as states face budget deficits, many legislatures are seriously considering holding public higher education institutions to new completion and transfer standards. Community colleges can no longer wait. Using institutional data, they must examine completion and transfer rates, decide if these are acceptable levels of completion, and explain why or determine a rate that they should aspire to achieve. At this time, the public has no basis for gauging the quality of community college completion rates, because there are no established standards (Nettles and Millett, 1999). As many senior institutions begin to establish ceilings on the number of freshman they can enroll, state legislators are forcing senior institutions and community colleges to work together to meet the needs of students who are attending community college for their first two years of study. Institutions should begin to seriously consider establishing transfer and completion rates that meet the needs of the students who attend the institutions and of their communities.

Recognize the institution's validation team. Instructors, counselors, and institutional mentors, to name a few, are access agents who are responsible for guiding and moving students along the educational pathway. It is critical to move these institutional agents toward viewing themselves as a validating team (see Rendón, 1999a). Institutions should start by taking inventory and recognizing those practices currently in place that serve to validate students on both academic and interpersonal levels. It is important to recognize best practices that are unique to an institution in order to build the team's strengths. Equip the team with the knowledge, skills, and awareness needed to support their ongoing efforts to foster students' personal development and social adjustment.

The bottom line is that community colleges need to change how they do business. Latinos will continue to turn to higher education as a vehicle for upward social, political, and economic mobility, and our social institutions will depend on community colleges to prepare, train, and support citizens who can sustain a diverse democracy. Creating and sustaining multicultural institutions, establishing completion and transfer standards, supporting research on Latino students, and recognizing institutions' validation teams need to be top priorities for community colleges concerned with facilitating student success.

References

Astin, A. W. *Minorities in American Higher Education*. (1st ed.) San Francisco: Jossey-Bass, 1982.

Astin, A. W. *What Matters in College?: Four Critical Years Revisited*. (1st ed.) San Francisco: Jossey-Bass, 1993.

Bensimon, E. M. (ed.). *Multicultural Teaching and Learning: Strategies for Change in Higher Education*. University Park, Penn.: National Center on Postsecondary Teaching, Learning, and Assessment, 1994.

Bensimon, E. M., and Riley, M. J. *Student Predisposition to Transfer: A Report of Preliminary Findings*. Los Angeles: Center for the Study of Community Colleges, 1984.

Brint, S. G., and Karabel, J. *The Diverted Dream: Community Colleges and the Promise of Educational Opportunity in America, 1900–1985*. New York: Oxford University Press, 1989.

Castaneda, C. "Transfer Rates Among Students from Rural, Suburban, and Urban Community Colleges: What We Know, Don't Know, and Need to Know." *Community College Journal of Research and Practice, 2002, 26,* 439–449.

Chronicle of Higher Education. "Chronicle of Higher Education Almanac." [http://chronicle.com/free/almanac/2002/index.htm]. 2002.

Cohen, A. M., and Brawer, F. B. *The American Community College*. (3rd ed.) San Francisco: Jossey-Bass, 1996.

Dougherty, K. J. "Community Colleges and Baccalaureate Attainment." *Journal of Higher Education, 1992, 63*(2), 188–214.

Fry, R. *Latinos in Higher Education: Many Enroll, Too Few Graduate*. Washington, D.C.: Pew Hispanic Center, 2002. [http://www.pewhispanic.org/site/docs/pdf/latinos inhighereducation-sept5–02.pdf]. Retrieved May 5, 2003.

Gandara, P. C. *Over the Ivy Walls: The Educational Mobility of Low-Income Chicanos*. Albany: State University of New York Press, 1995.

Gandara, P. *Puente Two-Year Evaluation*. Davis: University of California, 1996.

Hurtado, S., Milem, J. F., Clayton-Pedersen, A., and Allen, W. R. *Enacting Diverse Learning Environments: Improving the Climate for Racial/Ethnic Diversity in Higher Education*. ASHE-ERIC Higher Education Report, vol. 26, no. 8. Washington, D.C.: Graduate School of Education and Human Development, George Washington University, 1998a.

Hurtado, S., Milem, J. F., Clayton-Pedersen, A., and Allen, W. R. "Enhancing Campus Climates for Racial/Ethnic Diversity: Educational Policy and Practice." *Review of Higher Education, 1998b, 21*(3), 279–302.

Kane, T. J., and Rouse, C. E. "The Community College: Educating Students at the Margin Between College and Work." *Journal of Economic Perspectives, 9*(1), Winter 1995, pp. 63–84.

Kuh, G. D. "The Other Curriculum: Out-of-Class Experiences Associated with Student Learning and Personal Development." *Journal of Higher Education, 1995, 66*(2), 123–155.

National Center for Education Statistics. *Descriptive Summary of 1995–96 Beginning Postsecondary Students: 3 Years Later*. NCES 2000–154. Washington, D.C.: U.S. Department of Education, 2000. [http://nces.ed.gov/pubs2000/2000154.pdf]. Retrieved Jan. 20, 2004.

Nettles, M. T., and Millett, C. M. "Student Access in Community Colleges." A project of the W. K. Kellogg Foundation, American Association of Community Colleges, and Association of Community College Trustees. [http://www.aacc.nche.edu/Content/ NavigationMenu/ResourceCenter/Projects_Partnerships/Current/NewExpeditions/ IssuePapers/Student_Access_in_Community_Colleges.htm]. 1999. Retrieved Jan. 20, 2004.

Nora, A. "Two-Year Colleges and Minority Students' Educational Aspirations." In J. Smart (ed.), *Higher Education: Handbook of Theory and Research*. Vol. 9. New York: Agathon Press, 1993.

Rendón, L. "Fulfilling the Promise of Access and Opportunity: Toward a Vision of Collaborative Community Colleges for the 21st Century." A project of the W. K. Kellogg Foundation, American Association of Community Colleges, and Association of Community College Trustees. [http://www.aacc.nche.edu/Content/NavigationMenu/ResourceCenter/Projects_Partnerships/Current/NewExpeditions/IssuePapers/Fulfilling_the_Promise_of_Access_and_Opportunity.htm]. 1999a. Retrieved Jan. 20, 2004.

Rendón, L. "Toward a New Vision of the Multicultural Community College for the Next Century." In R. A. Rhoads (ed.), *Community Colleges as Cultural Texts*. Albany: State University of New York Press, 1999b.

Rendón, L., Justiz, M. J., and Resta, P. *Transfer Education in Southwest Border Community Colleges*. Columbia: University of South Carolina, 1988.

Rendón, L., and Nora, A. "A Synthesis and Application of Research on Hispanic Students in Community Colleges." *Community College Review*, 1989, 17(1), 17–24.

Rendón, L., and Nora, A. "Clearing the Pathway: Improving Opportunities for Minority Students to Transfer." In L. Bjork (ed.), *Minorities in Higher Education*. Phoenix, Ariz.: Oryx Press, 1994.

Rendón, L., and Valadez, J. "Qualitative Indicators of Hispanic Student Transfer." *Community College Review*, 1993, 20(4), 27–37.

Rhoads, R. A. "The Politics of Culture and Identity: Contrasting Images of Multiculturalism and Monoculturalism." In K. M. Shaw, R. A. Rhoads, and J. Valadez (eds.), *Community Colleges as Cultural Texts*. Albany: State University of New York Press, 1999.

Shaw, K. M., Rhoads, R. A., and Valadez, J. (eds.). *Community Colleges as Cultural Texts: Qualitative Explorations of Organizational and Student Culture*. Albany: State University of New York Press, 1999.

Suarez, A. L. "Forward Transfer: Strengthening the Educational Pipeline for Latino Community College Students." *Community College Journal of Research and Practice*, 2003, 27, 95–117.

Tinto, V. *Leaving College: Rethinking the Causes and Cures of Student Attrition*. Chicago: University of Chicago Press, 1987.

MAGADELENA MARTINEZ is a doctoral student at the Center for the Study of Postsecondary Education at the University of Michigan.

EDITH FERNÁNDEZ is a doctoral student at the Center for the Study of Postsecondary Education at the University of Michigan.

6

For Latino students, career development and planning includes the negotiation of family influences, peer expectations, and challenges as they develop career efficacy in work experiences as undergraduates. The model presented here outlines how students can benefit from a holistic perspective on the intersections of career and cultural identity.

Creating Meaning from Intersections of Career and Cultural Identity

Linda S. Gross

Clarifying one's occupation is an integral part of coming of age in contemporary American society. "What do you do?" or "Where do you work?" are central questions in nearly any initial dialogue between individuals. In the college setting, a significant amount of student identity is drawn from one's major. It is hard to imagine a discourse between college students that does not include the question "So, what's your major?" The college experience also facilitates students' exploration of their ethnic and racial identity as they struggle to find their place within larger social, economic, and political contexts. This chapter will explore the experiences of Latino business students at a large, predominantly white midwestern university, based on data and findings from a 2001 ethnographic study (Gross, 2001). As Latino students move into new worlds as a result of their academic and career choices, their aspirations are influenced by the sense of self-efficacy that they gain through interactions with peers and professional experiences in establishing a culturally relevant framework for who they are and who they will become.

The Demographic Context

The Bureau of Labor Statistics projects that Latinos will account for approximately 11.1 percent of the U.S. labor force in the year 2005, which represents the largest percentage increase of any workforce population (Fullerton, 1991). However, the gap in educational attainment continues to be pronounced for Latino Americans; only 10.6 percent of the Latino population holds a bachelor's degree, compared with 28.1 percent of the non-Latino population (Therrien and Ramirez, 2000). Among the Latino

NEW DIRECTIONS FOR STUDENT SERVICES, no. 105, Spring 2004 © Wiley Periodicals, Inc.

subgroups, there is considerable difference in educational attainment of bachelor's degrees: Mexican origin, 6.9 percent; Puerto Rican origin, 13 percent; Cuban origin, 23 percent; Central and South American origin, 10.6 percent (Therrien and Ramirez, 2000). Further, the occupational distribution of Latinos in the labor force is skewed toward "low paying, less stable, and more hazardous occupations" (Cordova and del Pinal, 1995, p. 17). Only 14.2 percent of Hispanics are employed in managerial or professional specialty occupations as compared to 35.1 percent of non-Hispanic whites for the same occupational group (Ramirez and de la Cruz, 2002). Therrien and Ramirez (2000) report that Mexican Americans (11.9 percent) are the least likely among Latino groups to work in managerial or professional occupations. These data more than suggest the presence of continuing educational and economic barriers for Latino Americans, especially Mexican Americans. Moreover, the projected growth of the Latino workforce and Latino underrepresentation in higher education may indicate a future gap in readiness for an increasingly technical labor force.

The struggle to integrate one's career aspirations within a society historically bound by barriers to educational access, economic resources, and political opportunities requires attention to factors that influence how Latino students develop career and vocational identities in cultural context. It is clear that existing research has been very limited in exploring career development in the context of social realities faced by Latino populations. Barriers arising from the lack of economic, educational, and political opportunities affect students' perceptions of themselves and their aspirations for the future. The dynamic and interactive nature of identity development through integration of social, cultural, and career aspects of the self provides the foundation for building our understanding of the career development process. By exploring the intersection of cultural and career identity in Latino students through their college experiences, we will gain insight into the complex process of how one integrates social and cultural expectations with one's aspirations for the future and enhance our ability as educators to enhance student development.

Negotiating the Gaps in Vocational and Career Theory

A continuing challenge in the fields of career development and vocational guidance has been to find a comprehensive theoretical frame through which to analyze and understand the individual's career development process. This challenge has produced a diverse body of propositions forming a somewhat fragmented and segmented theoretical base. One of the problems that is most evident on review of major career development research is the inadequacy of the various theoretical models in addressing differentiation based on gender, race, and class. These inadequacies are largely products of omission in that foundational theories such as those of Ginzburg, Axelrad, and

Figure 6.1. Conceptual Model for Intersections of Career and Cultural Identity

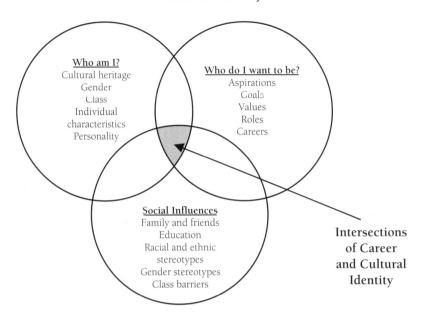

Herma (1951), Super (1957), and Holland (1966, 1985) were based on the study of primarily white, affluent college-bound men. Researchers seem to agree that career choice and development theory is underdeveloped with regard to multicultural populations and women (Arbona, 1990, 1995; Luzzo, 1992; Osipow and Littlejohn, 1995; Stitt-Gohdes, 1997).

Most career theory has focused on the questions "Who am I?" and "Who do I want to be?" either through personality and interest assessments or stage development approaches. A third dimension, social influences, is a critical mediating factor in identity and career development that can serve enabling or disabling functions, depending on the individual's sense of self arising from the first two dimensions. It is the interplay between the three dimensions that best explains individual identity and career development (see Figure 6.1). Any significant understanding of career development processes must consider how differences inherent in social, historical, economic, and political contexts affect cultural and gender groups. A contextual approach is especially important for Latino populations due to the heterogeneity of Latino subgroups (for example, Mexican Americans, Puerto Ricans, Cuban Americans, and Dominican Americans). Because the ethnic composition of Latino communities varies from campus to campus and region to region, it is critical to explore the unique characteristics of Latino communities as they have defined themselves in their campus and regional contexts.

It is also important to consider the concepts of identity, self-concept, and self-efficacy together, as they represent three important perspectives related to career and personal development. Erikson (1968) presents us with a psychosocial concept of identity, a sense of self that emerges through the interaction between the individual and his or her social world. Self-concept is an element of identity. Gottfredson (1981) defines self-concept as "one's view of oneself, one's view of who one is and who one is not. When projecting oneself into the future, self-concept also includes whom one expects or would like to be. People may or may not be consciously aware of the totality of different ways of seeing oneself, but they act on their beliefs about themselves" (p. 547). Bandura's concept of self-efficacy also focuses on beliefs about the self but adds an important perspective to the individual's mediation of psychological and social influences; he defines self-efficacy as "the belief in one's capabilities to organize and execute courses of action required to manage prospective situations" (1986, p. 37). Put simply, self-concept involves an individual's sense of self-worth; self-efficacy involves an individual's confidence in his or her ability to negotiate the challenges inherent in the larger social world. The remainder of this chapter will further explore the interplay of self-concept and self-efficacy by focusing on themes found in an ethnographic study of Latino business students at a large midwestern university (Gross, 2001).

Mastery Through Experience

Experiential learning through the job search process, work experience, and internships creates especially powerful mastery experiences that affect students' cultural and career self-efficacy. According to Bandura (1997), "mastery experiences are the most influential source of efficacy information because they provide the most authentic evidence of whether one can muster what it takes to succeed" (p. 80). As success grows through experience, so does students' confidence in their abilities and in their career path. Similarly, unsuccessful outcomes may cause students to rethink their career choices or hone them more succinctly. Students' career-related work experiences, especially internships, help to mold career identity as well as foster confidence and self-efficacy. A significant body of research suggests the impact of experiential learning and internships on students' career development. Thus, student affairs practitioners' efforts to create and encourage career-related experiential learning activities can have a positive impact on students' career development. Experiential learning may have an even more profound effect on students who are the first in their cultural community to choose or gain access to a particular career path. The following examples highlight the complex interplay of Latino students' hopes, fears, goals, and confidence with their experiences and provide insight into students' career aspirations and how students negotiate the intersections of their cultural and career identities.

Sara's (all student names in this chapter are pseudonyms) internship experiences highlight some typical concerns and fears that Latino students encounter in experiential learning. From first encounter to earned success, we can see a variety of intersections of cultural and career identity.

With several copies of a résumé she had written only the night before, Sara managed to get several interviews at the annual minority career fair. Her initial intention was just to get the experience of interviewing; however, her first interviews blossomed into her first internship offers. "I interviewed with several companies. I got job offers from all of them," she said. "I don't know how or why; they just liked something about me. I had no experience whatsoever."

Sara ended up choosing a major hotel chain because of name recognition and a location that would allow her to be near enough to her family but "far enough away where I still had that independence for the summer." Sara said it was a great experience for her, despite her initial concerns that other employees might think she only got the job to fill a minority quota.

> I was very shy about showing up to work the very first day. But nobody even knew. Nobody even mentioned anything or even cared. And there just so happened to be other students that were there . . . and they weren't minorities, so it kind of helped out. I felt really good about it.

That internship was Sara's first job, and she found herself sorting through some of her ideas about the hospitality field and the kinds of internship experiences she expected from an employer. By the end of her internship, she wasn't sure if she wanted to stay in the industry.

> I remember going through my exit interview and telling them all the things that I did not appreciate that happened to me. They are a great company and everything, but at that point in my life I wasn't too sure about it. And I was a little bit bitter because they made me do housekeeping work when that's not what I was there for. I wasn't there to learn how to dust light bulbs and make beds and clean toilets. And they only made me do it for a week, but I was just mad about it.

On the positive side, Sara felt the internship was helpful in that she had a rotation that gave her a broad exposure to the hotel industry. She said, "I didn't know what it was like to be in a managerial position or be a supervisor. I got to taste just a little bit of everything [and that helped] me figure out whether or not I wanted to do this for the rest of my life."

Sara's second internship experience took her to one of the largest hotels in Chicago. "And that place was huge when I was first there; I got lost for the first week every day. I couldn't make it from the locker room to the front desk [laughs]. I'd get lost." Assigned as a clerk to the front desk, she soon proved herself a quick study, learning the computerized property management system in record time. But the greatest lessons that Sara learned in the internship were about people and her ability to lead.

> Then one day I show up in the manager's uniform, and the clerks were pissed. They didn't know that I was an intern. One of them even said to me, "Who did you sleep with to get a promotion so quickly?" [laughs] So that was rough. But I learned how to deal with it, and I learned how to gain their respect, to get them to listen to me when I've got things for them to do. I learned a lot about myself; I learned a lot about what it is to have to keep that power distance between you as a manager and your employees, but also at the same time not to be their enemy.

By the end of the summer, Sara knew that she was valued, because no one wanted her to leave. She was asked to stay, but refused in favor of returning to school. She was surprised when she heard from them so quickly after she left, asking her to come back. Upon her return, Sara was assigned to a key role in the front office.

> The front office is the hub of everything, and if I don't do my job, then it is all going to fall apart. I'm supervising the staff of maybe twelve desk clerks and taking care of a two-thousand-room property. But I did it, and I did it well enough to where my superiors said that they were impressed.

Sara's experiences represent a coming of age with regard to her personal achievement potential and career development. In addition, like other students in their internships, she was able to teach the organization about the potential of interns to excel in their assignments. Sara is emphatic about the value of her internships: "I would never trade my internship experiences for anything. I have a much better idea of what it takes to succeed."

Olga's experience in a payment processing center of a utility company made a significant impact on her career development and professional confidence. After a couple of years, Olga earned more responsibility and managerial assignments. "I think my boss recognized my talent and my abilities, and he [had] me run meetings, staff meetings, head meetings with district managers and regional managers. . . . I really felt like a business person." Eventually she made a presentation to a few of the vice presidents. "They were really impressed. They said I did a really good job. The only thing they said was that I had to take the emotion out of my presentation, which is completely typical of me, because I'm so passionate about what I do," she laughs.

Bolstered by praise and opportunities, Olga eventually was managing processors in the payment center. "I increased the efficiency in decreasing the amount of workers that we needed, and I was just so proud of myself. Then, that's when I realized, 'You know what? I can do this. I can do it.'"

Even though she did not realize it when she was working at the payment center, her experiences predicted her eventual choice of a major in supply chain management. Like many other students, she knew little about specific fields in business, such as supply chain management, but she was able to rule out fields in which she felt a lack of fit. "I didn't like marketing. I didn't like finance. Didn't like accounting, etc. I didn't really like anything, and I didn't want to do general business. And econ, you know, in the College of Business, it's not like a business major per se. Hospitality business was out. Not working weekends and holidays." Olga discussed her experiences with her friend Juvé, who interned for a U.S. manufacturing company. "Juvé was studying supply chain, and we would just talk about it. . . . what it involved and everything like that, you know? And then I was like, 'that sounds like my work at [the payment center], and I really loved it. I love organizing stuff. I love having things work in a system and be efficient,' I said. 'I think I'd probably be really good at that.' And I think I am."

Olga was able to land an internship with a Latino manufacturing company before she graduated. "It was great," she says. "Now that I'm in my classes, my major classes, I can see how much knowledge I've gained just from witnessing everything in the company." Being able to integrate her classroom knowledge with her internship experiences helped Olga to affirm her skills and professional competence. She looks back on her internship with the manufacturing company as integral in providing a framework for her career and her education in supply chain management. "I can see how difficult it would be for students who haven't had internships, because you get all this knowledge. You know, you read and you learn, and take tests, but it doesn't mean anything. If you have a framework, you can correlate things." Olga is an excellent case example of the impact that internships and practical work experiences have on academic learning, self-confidence, and awareness of one's own career potential and opportunities. Being able to reinforce learning with experience and experience with learning is integral to students who are developing their career identity, but it is even more significant for Latino students as a building block to self-efficacy that can help them negotiate inequities as they attempt to gain access to and achieve success in professional worlds where they are underrepresented culturally.

Balancing Career and Cultural Identity

Latino students face some unique challenges in finding a balance between their career and cultural identities. For Latino students, being able to cope with ethnic stereotypes and prejudice, both in the workplace and on campus is a critical developmental task in addition to acquiring career knowledge and experience. The path to career success for Latino students often entails complex negotiations of personal values, social barriers, and cultural values as the following students' stories suggest.

Andres was a general business major toying with the idea of supply chain management when he got his first internship with a Japanese automaker. "It was a real job," he says. "I did the same thing that all the other people in my group did . . . purchase orders and getting requisitions." Andres learned a lot about the Japanese corporate world and even more about the challenges of being a Latino professional in a small, predominantly white town out of state. "It was a very bad living environment for me," he said, "a very, very racist town, very uninviting, unwelcoming. I was miserable." On his way home from work, he was pulling out of a shopping center when "this guy on this motorcycle like pulled up and said, 'Why don't you go back to Africa, you fuckin' nigger?'" Andres started to shout something back but decided it was safer just to drive away. "I've felt prejudice in my life," he says. "I mean, I *felt* it. I know what it's like. I just, I don't think I feel it all the time." To cope, he found himself driving three hours every weekend to go home or back to campus.

Although most of his work experiences were positive, Andres had to deal with a racial situation at the plant as well. Walking into work one morning around 7:30 A.M., Andres encountered an older white man walking out of the plant who asked him if he was going the wrong way.

> He said, 'Yeah, all you fucking minorities get the good jobs just because of the color of your skin.' I guess he assumed that I was going in to work the assembly line and I got an early shift, 'cuz there's like a ten-year waiting period.

Andres tried to analyze the situation, thinking, "If he logically would have looked at me, I was nineteen. He was fifty-four. Maybe I wasn't working on the assembly line, but who knows?" Andres was initially going to file a complaint against the worker. After some thought, he decided, "It wasn't worth my time or my effort to do anything about it. He was gonna think what he wanted to . . . but it didn't make me uncomfortable to go and work."

Andres refuses to let incidents such as these affect his work or career plans. Neither experience dissuaded him from pursuing his career in corporate America. "If anything," he said, "it limited my thought of the rest of humanity, but I don't think it had anything to do with my job or my job function. That was secure."

Many of the students expressed concerns about whether their internship offers were based on their minority status, wondering, "Did I get the job just because I'm a minority?" Alma laughs when she talks about the impact of the Latino explosion in popular culture, food, and the workplace. "Everybody wants the new thing, and the new thing is Latinos," she says. "Everybody just wants to be a part of the fad, and the fad right now is Latinos. Sometimes I almost think, 'Do they want me just because I'm Latino or because I can really do it?'" Luisa, a senior marketing major, believes that employers assumed she was Hispanic because of her name and her student activities. "No one's treated me any differently in a bad way because I've been Hispanic, but I've noticed people have just given me more opportunities," she says. "But they are only opportunities."

After Andres's experience with the Japanese automaker, his view of opportunities based on race and culture is markedly different. Realizing that his first internship offer may well have been based on his ethnic background, he's quite clear about how he would respond in a similar situation. "If I was offered the internship this summer, and I went there and I saw that they had twenty-five interns and eighteen were minorities, I think I would quit, because you're only hiring me based on the fact that I'm a minority." Andres expresses a common theme that other students talked about with regard to their ethnic background and their career achievement and opportunity:

> I guess it's good in some aspects if it's gonna get me to where I want to be in life, but it's not a crutch to me. Being Mexican is not a crutch. If there is somebody better qualified who's white, hire that person. I don't want you to help me because I'm Mexican. I don't need your help. . . . I don't want anybody handing anything to me. I don't need anything handed to me. I'll work for what I get, and I'll be happy with that.

Andres's response to racial and ethnic challenges in the workplace draws on the confidence he has in his ability to work and to achieve in his career. The opportunity to work and prove oneself in the workplace is an important expression of one's career and cultural identity. As Bandura (1997) has suggested, success that arises from achievement is the most powerful influence on individual efficacy.

Latino students who choose conservative professions, such as business and engineering, may also have to cope with difficult criticisms from co-ethnic peers on campus who challenge their connection to their cultural community. Amanda was unsure about how much her peers in the Latino student community respected her, especially those that were involved in political groups. Although she actively mentors youth in the community and has arranged numerous community service activities with other Latino business students, she senses that her commitment to the community is questioned by her non–business student peers:

> When I tell them [Latino peers] I'm a business major, . . . they don't see that as helping the community, because . . . I'm going to be in the corporate world. But I think I am helping the community. I see it as helping 'cause I'm getting up in the corporate world. There's not that big of a population of Chicanos in the corporate world, and it's not going to happen unless [more of us] start joining that workforce. I don't know if they're that open to realizing that what I'm going to be doing is also helping the Latino community.

Amanda is typical of many Latino students who cope with co-ethnic criticism. Their underlying fear is expressed when they ask, "Am I really a sellout? Am I betraying my culture in favor of my career success?" The reality that this fear exists stems from the history and contemporary influence of social structures that have limited access to opportunity such that those from some cultural backgrounds cannot reconcile their cultural heritage with professional success. As Latino students experience intersections of career and cultural identity through their college lives, they mediate new ideas and social practices that they encounter along the way. In doing so, they create new meanings for themselves in what it means to be a successful Latino professional. They tend to weave their values and vision of family, cultural heritage, career achievement, and community into the fabric of their lives, linking their professional achievement to the advancement of their cultural communities.

Strength and Efficacy Through Community

As members of one of the smallest cultural populations enrolled in a large, predominantly white midwestern university, Latino students find that being part of a culturally relevant professional student organization is an important influence in their career and cultural identities. The absence of cultural role models on the business faculty and the relative absence of cultural support for Latinos within the minority program in the college left co-ethnic peer associations as the only viable means of cultural support for the students in the study. All but three students in the study were active members of the Hispanic Business Association (HBA), although all students in the study had attended a meeting or participated in an HBA event. "We're friends first, but we're organized and we take care of business," said a former officer of the organization.

HBA grew out of Latino outreach efforts by a minority support program housed in the College of Business. However, in 1994, eleven students attended the National Hispanic Leadership Conference in Austin, Texas. The impact of the conference on the students was "overwhelming." Christian explains, "It was the amount of people there, dressing up in a suit and trying to be professional, and having a résumé. It was the business world, and it felt great. I loved it. I felt like the people that we went down there with, the group members, we got stronger, and we built business relationships." The national conference is run by the National Hispanic Business Association (NHBA), a student-run organization founded by students at the University of Texas at Austin. When that first group of students came back to campus, they became the first chartered chapter of the organization in their state. The connection to NHBA helped give the group a structure and a business purpose to attend the leadership conference each year.

The national conference has had an inspiring effect on all the students in the study who have been able to attend. Jamie talks about his first experience of going to Austin and the impact of being part of a conference with six hundred Latino business students from across the country: "There's fifteen people, and then you got down there and there was a huge convention center of people just like you and all working to do the same thing. You don't think that big sometimes. You see your little group, and, you know, that's it. But there's so many more people out there that are doing the same thing." Asked if the conference influenced his decision to major in business, Jamie is quick to respond. "It didn't affect my decision on business. It did affect my decision on how much harder I'm gonna work, that you really got to get above the average guy."

The conference's impact on Alma was to help her to realize new possibilities and gain confidence in herself and her college career. Through the conference and career fairs, she has cultivated good relationships with some of the corporate representatives whom she "always sees" at conferences. She's astonished that they know her. "They'll go, like 'Hi Alma, what's up?'" Alma gushes. "Never would I have thought that they would recognize me like that or remember my name."

The professional contacts that students make at conferences and career fairs are significant, but at the national conference, networking among peers is an important objective of all of the students who attend. Carlos explains that networking is building a future:

> You get to network with colleagues from different universities, from different regions that don't have the same challenges that you do. You really get to learn what's going on in different areas of the nation. This is something you have to learn how to do, because you're not only going to be dealing with the midwest perspective. You're going to be dealing with what's going on in the Southwest, East Coast, maybe, down in Montana. Who knows? You've really got to understand the people and why they make decisions.

The connection to the national Hispanic business community is significant. Individual students found new possibilities for their future in business and gained vital perspectives on the national Hispanic business community and the world outside campus. But perhaps most important is the effect the organization has had on the students' individual and collective self-efficacy. "You know, it makes you feel good. It really does," Carlos said, "knowing that you're part of this great organization that's run by students that gets national recognition. It makes you proud of what you are and what you accomplish, and what you can accomplish down the road."

Exposure to the national organization created a stronger, more cohesive group on campus. Alma describes it as a "family environment. You feel a lot closer to people that are there. And these are people that you will always keep in touch with, you know, forever." For Julio, that sense of family was important in how HBA members pulled together to support each other socially, academically, and professionally. "I formed a lot of study groups with them," he said, taking pride in the way he and his peers helped each other out. Alma concurred:

It has helped me a lot to learn about what business is and what it is supposed to be and what it will be in the future. . . . HBA has really put most of those things into perspective, as well as giving me another support group to discuss some things that you might be embarrassed or shy to talk about in a huge classroom of five hundred people. Just like résumé things or about how to dress for an interview or how to speak to someone or when you have an interview with them.

The group's responsibility to the Latino community extends beyond just its own membership. HBA has been committed to hosting groups of college-bound migrant students from Texas, reaching out to Cuban refugees, and preparing care packages for fellow Latino students and low-income families, as well as mentoring Latino middle school students. Socially, members of the group often attend parties together and maintain contact with alumni from the organization who have graduated. Upper-division students regularly share stories and updates on the successes of HBA alumni who have graduated. A former officer and well-known alumnus states that the most important role of HBA for its alumni and members is "reaching out to our brothers and sisters to help them achieve what we have achieved."

The supportive community that HBA members have created is an especially powerful one. Not only does HBA create a safe place in which students can explore their cultural heritage and career identity, but it provides them with a sense of collective efficacy as they help one another to reach their goals in college and beyond. In the absence of available role models, the group created its own role models within the group itself, with members building on one another's success through vicarious experiences and other social learning processes. All of the students in the study expressed the desire to give something back, to make a difference in their family and their community, and most equated that with personal achievement and financial independence.

Recommendations for Practitioners and a Model for Student Development

So what do these themes represent in terms of practical implications for student affairs and career services professionals? The findings of the study support the idea that peer associations that combine both career and cultural activities foster both individual and collective efficacy. This suggests that educators may be able to facilitate the growth of collective efficacy through advising and support of professional and major-related student organizations such as the Society of Hispanic Professional Engineers and the Hispanic National Bar Association. Collective efficacy through career-oriented peer associations is especially salient for groups that have limited co-ethnic role models in college or in their intended profession. Further studies on the effects of professional peer associations, career experiences, and internships on minority student success in fields such as business, engineering, and medicine would be particularly interesting.

A number of pragmatic implications for working with first-generation college students arose from the study. First-generation college students in the study tended to have a limited understanding of career options available to them and the work entailed in given majors. This suggests that it may be very important for first-generation and low-income students to participate in experiential learning opportunities, such as internships, professional conferences, or site visits, in order to explore their career choices. Evidence in the study suggested that student mastery of career-related experiences enhanced student success in their career field and increased academic interest in their major.

The study also provided evidence that mastery experiences, such as internships, enhance self-efficacy and the potential for career success. Employers tend to look for three key elements in evaluating prospective employees: (1) capacity for learning, generally measured through an individual's educational attainment; (2) experience related to their intended job function and general problem solving, as is evident from the rise of behavior-based interviews and pre-employment activities; and (3) leadership, generally evaluated by reviewing an individual's initiative and achievements in extracurricular involvement in organizations and campus and community activities. Consider these elements through the lens of current career theory. Super gives us the concept of career maturity. Career maturity refers to the level at which students accomplish developmental career tasks, formulate career plans, and understand the parameters of their chosen career (Super, 1957, 1984). Career maturity is vitally dependent on experiential learning and mastery through self-reflection. As is evident from the study, students involved in professional organizations and internships gained greater confidence, career certainty, and maturity through these developmental experiences during their college years. Bandura's (1997) concept of self-efficacy through mastery experiences is equally important in understanding the student's career development process, because it provides a critical theoretical foundation for the elements of experience and self-reflective learning. If we consider the saliency of mastery experiences in the study along the lines of learning, experience, and leadership, a clear model emerges (see Figure 6.2).

Imagine the core of this model to be the essential elements of the self (identity, values goals, and social influences) as delineated in the Conceptual Model for Intersections of Career and Cultural Identity (Figure 6.1). Surrounding the core are the three elements of mastery critical to career development and workplace success: the capacity for continual learning; work and life experiences leading to maturity; and leadership, which relates directly to individual initiative. A circle of continual self-reflection powers the individual's ongoing development. The significance of the model is that

Figure 6.2. Career Learning Model

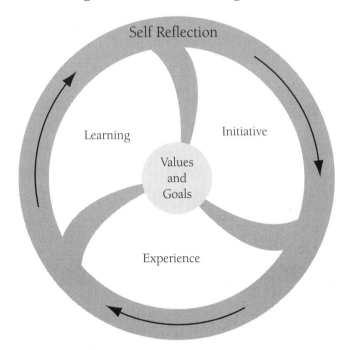

it provides a framework for understanding a complex and multidimensional development process. The importance of such a framework is echoed in Olga's earlier reflection on her mastery experiences in college: "You get all this knowledge. You know, you read and you learn, and take tests, but it doesn't mean anything. If you have a framework, you can correlate things." A dynamic career development process requires a model in which you can see how the pieces fit together even if they are continually changing.

The most critical role practitioners can play in facilitating Latino student development is by creating culturally relevant opportunities for students to reflect on the meaning of and the connections between their curricular and cocurricular experiences. It is not enough to just take classes, be part of a student organization, or complete an internship. It is by engaging in self-reflection that students are able to understand the dynamic components of their career development process and create meaning for themselves within the context of their social and cultural worlds.

References

Arbona, C. "Career Counseling Research and Hispanics: A Review of the Literature." *The Counseling Psychologist,* 1990, *18*(2), 300–323.

Arbona, C. "Theory and Research on Racial and Ethnic Minorities: Hispanic Americans." In F.T.L. Leong (ed.), *Career Development and Vocational Behavior of Racial and Ethnic Minorities.* Mahwah, N.J.: Erlbaum, 1995.

Bandura, A. *Social Foundations of Thought and Action: A Social Cognitive Theory*. Upper Saddle River, N.J.: Prentice Hall, 1986.

Bandura, A. *Self-Efficacy: The Exercise of Control*. New York: W. H. Freeman, 1997.

Cordova, C., and del Pinal, J. *Hispanics—Latinos: Diverse People in a Multicultural Society*. (Special report). Washington, D.C.: National Association of Hispanic Publications, 1995.

Erikson, E. H. *Identity: Youth and Crisis*. (1st ed.) New York: Norton, 1968.

Fullerton, H. N. "Labor Force Projections: The Baby Boom Moves On." *Monthly Labor Review*, 1991, *114*, 31–44.

Ginzberg, E. G., Axelrad, S., and Herma, J. L. *Occupational Choice. An Approach to General Theory*. New York: Columbia University Press, 1951.

Gottfredson, L. S. "Circumscription and Compromise: A Developmental Theory of Occupational Aspirations." *Journal of Counseling Psychology*, 1981, 28(6), 545–579.

Gross, L. S. "Intersections of Career and Cultural Identity in Mexican American College Students." Unpublished doctoral dissertation, Michigan State University, East Lansing, 2001.

Holland, J. *The Psychology of Vocational Choice*. Waltham, Mass.: Blaisdell, 1966.

Holland, J. *Making Vocational Choices: A Theory of Careers*. Upper Saddle River, N.J.: Prentice Hall, 1985.

Luzzo, D. A. "Ethnic Group and Social Class Differences in College Students' Career Development." *Career Development Quarterly*, 1992, 41(2), 161–173.

Osipow, S., and Littlejohn, E. "Toward a Multicultural Theory of Career Development: Prospects and Dilemmas." In F.T.L. Leong (ed.), *Career Development and Vocational Behavior of Racial and Ethnic Minorities*. Mahwah, N.J.: Erlbaum, 1995.

Ramirez, R., and de la Cruz, P. *The Hispanic Population in the United States: March 2002*. Current Population Reports, P20–545. Washington, D.C.: U. S. Census Bureau, 2002. [http://www.census.gov/prod/2003pubs/p20–545.pdf]. Retrieved Feb. 4, 2004.

Stitt-Gohdes, W. L. *Career Development: Issues of Race, Gender, and Class*. Information Series No. 371. Columbus, Ohio: ERIC Clearinghouse on Adult, Career and Vocational Education, 1997.

Super, D. E. *Vocational Development: A Framework for Research*. New York: Teachers College Press, 1957.

Super, D. E. "Career and Life Development." In D. Brown and L. Brooks (eds.), *Career Choice and Development: Applying Contemporary Theories to Practice*. San Francisco: Jossey-Bass, 1984.

Therrien, M., and Ramirez, R. *The Hispanic Population in the United States: March 2000*. Current Population Reports, P20–535. Washington, D.C.: U.S. Census Bureau, 2000. [http://www.census.gov/prod/2001pubs/p20–535.pdf]. Retrieved Feb. 4, 2004.

LINDA S. GROSS *is associate director of career development services at Michigan State University.*

Research shows that Latino students are grossly underrepresented in higher education. In this chapter, however, we show how family, community, and institutional partnerships can be an evidence-based practice for faculty and student affairs professionals who wish to increase Latino participation and graduation rates.

Support Programs That Work

Liliana Mina, José A. Cabrales, Cynthia M. Juarez, Fernando Rodriguez-Vasquez

For decades, major journal articles, conference presentations, and doctoral dissertations have centered on the academic achievement of college students of color. Notwithstanding, most analyses of academic achievement and students of color are limited to the study of grades, test scores, grade point average, and other pre-enrollment characteristics. There is no doubt that academic success in college depends on a solid and rigorous high school curriculum; however, for Latino students, academic readiness is only one component that is necessary for a successful collegiate experience. For many Latino college students to be successful, the interplay between family, community, peers, and the institution must create an environment that is conducive to a positive experience.

This chapter focuses on alternative evidence of success by moving beyond traditional research article formats. Instead, we provide personal and autobiographical perspectives on our experiences as Latino undergraduates. Our stories are very personal. We share various conceptions of ourselves in the hope of helping student service professionals to better understand the influence that institutional programs, campus organizations, mentors, and leadership opportunities may have on Latino student success.

While there are some major frameworks for examining and understanding the collegiate experiences of students of color, we believe that our narratives provide the most authentic source of information. Rather than providing snapshots of our lives, we focus on particular individuals and experiences that had a major impact on our academic journey.

We are indebted to Anna Maria Ortiz for her never-ending support and commitment to Latino student success.

NEW DIRECTIONS FOR STUDENT SERVICES, no. 105, Spring 2004   © Wiley Periodicals, Inc.

José's Story

Supporting my desire to attend a four-year university was the most fearful decision my parents had to make. As with any first-time experience, my parents did not know what to expect and were frightened at the risk of sending me to a private university where tuition was approximately $25,000 per year. At first, my mother was hesitant to take the risk and asked me if I had inquired about a local community college. I was devastated by her suggestion, because I had worked so hard in high school to attend a reputable university. After some soul searching, I put myself in my parents' position and understood that it would be a great sacrifice for them to send me to a university not knowing if I was going to succeed. Therefore, once I was admitted to the school of my choice, I knew I had to succeed.

During my sophomore year, I became involved with a couple of student organizations and campus programs. I was very fortunate to meet a woman recently hired as an admissions counselor for Latino students. She asked if I would like to assist her with outreach and recruitment programs. I was very flattered and gladly accepted her invitation. Working in admissions was a great experience, because I was able to work with a counselor who actively recruited in communities where there was a significant number of Latinos. Through her efforts, undergraduate admissions went through a transformation in its recruitment of Latino students. Not only did the department hire an individual who was passionate about the advancement of students, but she was instrumental in my involvement in a number of programs specifically designed to meet the needs of Latino students and their families.

For instance, she created bilingual parent receptions, which were held at the homes of parents of current Santa Clara University (SCU) students. The receptions were created to answer any questions that parents might have as their children embarked on the journey of higher education. Like my parents, other parents were very hesitant to send their children away to Santa Clara University either because of the fear that they would fail or because they were the first child in their family to attend an institution of higher learning. A significant number of Latino applicants were from areas such as East San Jose, Redwood City, Salinas, and Watsonville, so we scheduled our receptions in these areas in order to establish communication between Spanish-speaking parents and the university. My family was fortunate to host the first Watsonville reception, which six families attended. The admissions counselor, my parents, and I answered questions from parents on topics ranging from the safety of their children to what student services were available to them. My parents were very excited about hosting the reception, because it was something they wished had been available to them before I attended Santa Clara University. The program served dual purposes, educating future parents about the college-going experience and building stronger connections between current parents and the university.

Working on campus also gave me the opportunity to become a member of Latino organizations. I was an active member in MEChA-El Frente as well as Chicanos and Latinos in Engineering and Sciences at SCU (ChALESS). As an active member, I was able to help in annual activities that MEChA-El Frente hosted, such as Cinco de Mayo and Misa de la Virgen de Guadalupe (Celebration of the Virgin Guadalupe). In addition, a group of twelve young men and I founded a chapter of Sigma Lambda Beta International Fraternity, Inc. Our initial intention in creating this brotherhood was to increase the resources available to students of color on campus. We accomplished this, and members were also able to increase their participation in campus and community activities as well as work closely with other student organizations. Through my working experiences with the university, I became an advocate for other students. I learned how to work with different departments across the university and with community organizations. Before long, the fear and risk that my parents had felt as I began Santa Clara University were overshadowed by pride and accomplishment.

The experience that I had in working with the admissions counselor and other faculty and staff across the university enabled me to become an active part of the campus community. In addition, it gave me the courage I needed to delve into the community and serve as a catalyst for change.

Cynthia's Story

I am the daughter of two first-generation Mexican Americans. I have two sisters, and together we are the first in our family to pursue college degrees. I am grateful for all the sacrifices that my parents have made for me to attend university. My parents are very proud of me. When I entered the University of Texas at El Paso, which we affectionately call UTEP, I was timid and unable to verbalize my opinions. I was doubtful of my abilities. I spent my days going to and from classes and then home. Weeks often passed without my uttering a single word. One day, a friend of my sister's came and told me about a three-day leadership camp that was being held on campus. Although I was very reluctant to attend, the experience helped me to see that I was a valuable and capable person. The leadership camp was more than an exercise in leadership training; attending the camp changed my life.

It is interesting to note that although this camp was not designed specifically for Latino students, UTEP is 70 percent Latino, which helped me to see other Latino students taking active roles as leaders. It was a dynamic opportunity for me to see students of color taking leadership roles and responsibilities, and that helped me to envision myself taking these same roles in the future.

My first step after attending the leadership camp was to get involved in school activities. Interestingly, I felt compelled to join the office that put together the leadership camp. I spent what seemed like an eternity outside the door of the Student Development Center before I finally got up the nerve to enter it. However, the moment I walked in, I knew my life would be different. Slowly, I became an instrumental member of this department. I would go by every day and just see what was going on. I became like a fly on the wall, and soon I was spending so much time there that I started to get involved in the activities they planned.

I first worked with the wellness advocacy program. This program was designed to inform the university community of the advantages of being a well-rounded individual. It was through this program that I was given my first taste of student programming. We planned many student activities that coincided with national events such as Safe and Sober Spring Break, The Great American Smokeout, and World AIDS Day. In addition to giving me programming experience, I felt that the Student Development Center helped to set the foundation for an active interest and commitment to my personal development.

In turn, I began to care very deeply about the Student Development Center and the university as a whole. I immersed myself in the daily activities of the department. I began to help not only with the programs but with the daily duties of keeping the office functioning. I would answer phones, make copies, cover the reception desk, and on occasion I was left in charge while the staff attended meetings, retreats, or campus functions.

During my tenure, the Student Development Center began a small internship program designed to help students from our area who were interested in student services careers after graduation. I ended up being part of the group of students participating in the pilot internship program. It was through this internship that I was afforded the opportunity to work in a number of leadership roles in many programs on campus. I was responsible for helping to maintain records for more than a hundred student organizations, as well as helping to design and implement the leadership seminars that were taught throughout the academic year.

I worked at the center for the better part of four years. It is the place where I found my avocation. I am no longer a scared and timid child. I am a confident adult who knows her heart and her head. With this new confidence, I have made many changes in my life, the first of which was improving my self-esteem. I began to like the person that I was, and with that came a newfound respect for being fit in body, mind, and spirit.

One aspect of my education at UTEP that I feel was invaluable and possibly the most influential factor in my college experience was the interaction that I had with many mentors on campus. I was fortunate to find individuals within the institution who not only took the time to foster my growth but often did it at the expense of their free time.

In particular, there were three mentors from my undergraduate years who spent countless hours working with me. Joseph Aguirre not only helped get me more involved with school but also took the time to get to know my family quite well. I know that his effort to get involved with them helped my parents to support the decisions I made.

Sylvia Juaregui was one of the first young, strong, intellectual, and empowered Latinas that I came to know and interact with. She was the first role model that I actually could see myself emulating. Sylvia pushed me to become my own woman and helped me to see that it was worth the time and effort to develop my own identity—that I was worth it. She did not want to create a carbon copy of herself; she was deeply invested in seeing me become my own woman. She spent countless hours helping me with everything from learning how to care for myself (clothes, makeup, hairdos) to developing a personal and professional ethic. Like Joseph, she got deeply involved with my family, and we have come to care about each other like family as well. Forever she will be a sister to me.

Finally, there was Gary Edens, whose quiet reserve helped to guide me in innumerable ways. Although he is not Latino, living and working in the Southwest has aided him greatly in acquiring the unique perspective that comes from working with the Latino population. Gary never gave me an opportunity to think of failure. The fact that he always trusted me to do well and never micromanaged the way in which I accomplished my goals has been invaluable. Gary aided me in school and in the work that I performed there, and he helped my family to see that I needed to not only graduate but to become independent from them. While my family may not have understood it at the time, in hindsight they see the benefits that my leaving their house has provided. Gary helped me to find the courage to leave. He was the first person who entrusted me with my own identity and left me to sculpt my own future.

Although I cannot quantify how much I learned as an undergraduate at UTEP, I firmly believe that the student affairs professionals who took an interest in me made a significant contribution to the development of not just my talents but also my character. Their willingness to get involved with more than the side of me they saw at school dramatically influenced the person that I have become. This personal investment in me, coupled with the fact that UTEP is a Hispanic-serving institution, gave me the opportunity to see Latino role models within the institution and has enabled me to visualize my success and ability to compete with others.

Fernando's Story

Imagine living in a community that is best known for its failures. Imagine growing up in a community whose name is synonymous with violence and riots. To grow up in Watts is to know that a bullet can find you before you find yourself, before you attend your prom or obtain a driver's license. Yet in a community associated with violence and tragedy, my immigrant parents from Nayarit, Mexico, managed to raise socially responsible and productive children. Through their hard work, consistent guidance, and support, I graduated from high school and enrolled in East Los Angeles College (ELAC).

Initially, I was only interested in attending college to help my family financially, but while attending ELAC, I joined MECHA, which encouraged and promoted my cultural heritage through a number of community and educational activities. After two years at ELAC, I transferred to San Diego State University (SDSU). It took a year to fully acclimate to my new environment. Without the support of my Latino peers, I would have had a difficult time making it through college.

While concerns are frequently expressed about how membership in Greek organizations affects academic performance, my SDSU experience paints a different picture. For instance, participation in mandatory study hours is common in many fraternities and sororities. In fact, while I was attending SDSU, the fraternity and the sorority with the highest grade point average were both Latino. Latino students were not just socially integrated into the campus community, but we were also very academically motivated. For many Latino students, membership in a Greek organization provides unity and creates a sense of belonging on campus. With camaraderie and support from my peer group, I felt that I had a better chance of completing my education and, consequently, gaining the confidence and encouragement to attend graduate school.

One of the most important activities for my fraternity was serving as mentors to high school students and sponsoring College and Career Days at local high schools. Through our involvement with our community, we presented other options besides joining a gang. Not only did we serve as role models for members of our community, but our efforts served as a recruitment mechanism for reaching students of color. Our goal was to encourage students to complete high school and earn a college education.

Another valuable community service project performed by our fraternity was a tutoring program for elementary students whose parents attended adult education courses to improve their English-speaking skills. We also worked with disabled children at a local church every Sunday. Other Latino fraternities and sororities volunteered at homeless shelters and food banks. We felt that the community was very important to us, and to our surprise, many community members appreciated our dedication to service.

I believe that our involvement helped to dispel preconceived notions and prejudices about ethnic groups and college students in general. Besides serving on numerous campus projects and activities, many Latino members of Greek organizations served as translators for various academic departments throughout the campus. Through these activities, we saw ourselves as a viable, integral part of the university and reinforced our pride in our heritage and cultural values at the same time.

My involvement through my Latino fraternity helped me to realize that mentors are invaluable to young people. My mentoring experience led me to seek a faculty mentor at SDSU, because I felt that I needed someone for academic, social, and emotional support. As I began to search for candidates, I felt that I would have many people to choose from; however, that was not case. I spoke with a variety of professors and staff members, and it appeared that most faculty members were too busy to get involved. I was very disappointed and frustrated that I was unsuccessful in connecting with a faculty member at a major university. As I examined other possibilities, I thought about my peers as potential candidates. I had never considered them before, but it turned out to be the best decision that I made while attending SDSU. I asked one of the senior members of my fraternity if he would be my mentor, and he gladly accepted. While I was looking for support in the college community it became evident that my support system was all around me; Nu Alpha Kappa was there when others turned away. The lessons here are that Latino peers are just as valuable as faculty and staff, and that Latino Greek organizations are important components in the college environment.

Liliana's Story

I was born in Cali, Colombia, the eldest of three children. My parents emigrated to Detroit when I was about eleven years old. Three major events mark my cross-cultural transition to the United States. Within days of our arrival, my sister and I were enrolled in school. At school, no one spoke Spanish, so I had to learn English on my own. After school, I completed my lessons in Spanish and received English instruction from my dad. In school, all I could do was math (as long as there weren't any story problems!). The isolation I felt gradually began to subside as the other kids became aware that I was actually smart. I managed to win the school's spelling bee after the first year. Little did anyone know that instead of watching TV or playing after school, I studied every night until ten or eleven o'clock.

My second cross-cultural transition came when we moved to the lower east side of Detroit. A small Latino community, which also became our extended family, quickly embraced us. My friends were Cubans, Mexicans, Puerto Ricans, and anyone else whose family spoke a language other than English at home. As Latinos, we celebrated traditional holidays together, carpooled to school, and worshiped in the same church. Through high school, I also participated in Detroit's Latin American festivals by selling tamales and helping with folkloric presentations. Because of a loving and supportive community that made sure that my cultural identity stayed intact, I was able to do well in school.

My third cross-cultural transition was a traumatic yet life-changing experience. I decided to go away to college over a hundred miles from my family and friends. Once again, I was alone, surrounded by people who did not look like me or think like me and by professors who constantly questioned whether I belonged. Not one professor made the attempt to pronounce my name correctly, and of course I refused to answer to the

American version of my name. Needless to say, after the first quarter I was ready to go home.

My saving grace came when my financial aid was canceled due to a clerical error. I went to the financial aid office, and after standing in line for what seemed like hours, I started to cry. One of the staff members saw me, grabbed my forms, and to my surprise, pronounced my name correctly. I looked up and realized I was seeing a Latino in front of me. Between sobs, in Spanish I told him about all the hardships and loneliness I felt. Within a few minutes, he not only took care of my problem but also advised me to take courses with the few Latino professors and other faculty of color on campus. Meeting these faculty members made it so much easier for me to integrate into campus life.

I was soon baby-sitting for many of them, attending potlucks, stopping by their offices for chats, and meeting other students from similar backgrounds. Once again, I became part of a community that understood what I was experiencing and helped to make my transition to college more positive and successful. I continue to be friends with many of the faculty and staff that had such an impact on my undergraduate experience. Many of them now hold prominent positions at other academic institutions and federal agencies. It was their compassion, role modeling, and never-ending support, along with the encouragement of others, that propelled me to apply for my first professional position, working with students of color as an academic guidance counselor.

Working in the Office of Supportive Services at Michigan State University as an academic guidance counselor was a challenging but rewarding experience. Prior to my employment, individuals holding my position had been Chicanos and Mexican Americans, since most of the students that I would be working with were of that background. Fortunately, the director of the program had had the foresight to have four Chicano students on the interview committee. After a rigorous interview session, which entailed sharing my college experience, the students felt that I understood the issues they faced and that I would be able to assist them.

As an academic guidance counselor, networking and receiving support from other Latino professionals on campus really helped me to grow professionally and personally. I became treasurer of the Chicano Latino Staff Professional Association, and was involved in many activities designed to increase the presence and visibility of Latinos on campus. For instance, in cooperation with other support service programs, I was involved in the development of a number of academic, leadership, and cultural enrichment retreats for Latino students.

One of our most memorable retreats involved spending time with Julian Samora, the first Mexican American to receive a doctorate in sociology and anthropology. I can still remember the profound impact that Professor Samora's presence had on the students, especially his words of encouragement for those students interested in pursuing graduate degrees in Mexican American studies. After hearing that one young man aspired to earn a graduate degree but doubted his abilities for graduate work, a mentor was assigned to the student to help him develop a timetable and a long-term plan.

It was during our small discussion groups, oral history lessons, and sharing of personal aspirations that we affirmed and celebrated our customs, traditions, and unique cultural characteristics as Latinos and Americans. Since interaction on a daily basis with other Latinos on campus was fairly minimal, the retreats served as a way to connect with and support one another. A college education involved more than just attending class, getting good grades, and selecting the right major or career. By coming together, we committed to taking action, to doing something about what we most cherished—family and community.

Serving Our Community

Our bittersweet journeys as undergraduate students have not been forgotten. Instead, we dedicate ourselves to the service of others. We are committed to increasing the pool of Latinos in higher education by working and volunteering in student services programs and community organizations that specifically address the needs of first-generation and other historically underserved communities.

One subject that receives little attention in the higher education literature is the factors that influence Latino excellence in academia. Perhaps it is because the rewards achieved are internal and often intangible—that is, we succeed because in doing so, we reclaim our histories, our families, our communities, and our heritages. As students, we know that any success achieved is built on the shoulders of others. We realize that obtaining a college education comes with specific responsibilities to our community. Hence, the factors influencing our academic achievement in college are the desire and responsibility to assist in bridging the economic gap and increasing the level of educational attainment for our community.

Faculty and student services professionals can help Latino students make the most of college by understanding our values and personally involving individual students in the daily life of the institution. Accordingly, we recommend the following initiatives:

- Provide admissions and other information in English and Spanish.
- Portray Latino students and their families in recruitment brochures and other institutional publications, including Web sites.
- Involve Latino parents, community leaders, and community organizations in institutional recruitment efforts.
- Increase Latino visibility in student staffing, especially in orientation programs, academic departments, and administrative offices.

- Create leadership training and leadership positions specifically for Latino students in Latino and campuswide organizations.
- Identify and develop alternative outcomes indicators for student success (leadership, cocurricular activities, or change in a student's knowledge, attitude, or behavior resulting from a program or activity).
- Identify, mentor, and prepare current Latino students for professional positions in student affairs.
- Integrate Latino research, textbooks, and culture in course content.
- Learn about our diverse cultures and cultural practices by bringing in speakers from Latin America, Central America, the Caribbean, and different parts of the United States.

Our narratives indicate that one of the keys to Latino college student success is to build strong university-family-community partnerships. Our experiences suggest that Latino students develop certain characteristics that enable us to succeed in college. Although we are relatively small in number, by showing a special interest in us, faculty and student affairs professionals can help us succeed in college. We can then return to our respective communities and reach out and support others in attaining higher education.

LILIANA MINA is a doctoral candidate at Michigan State University in the department of Higher, Adult, and Lifelong Education.

JOSÉ A. CABRALES is pursuing a master's degree in student affairs administration at Michigan State University.

CYNTHIA M. JUAREZ is pursuing a master's degree in student affairs administration at Michigan State University.

FERNANDO RODRIGUEZ-VASQUEZ is pursuing a master's degree in student affairs administration at Michigan State University.

8

This synthesis of the volume offers recommendations that will help student services personnel to facilitate the success of Latino students in higher education.

Promoting the Success of Latino Students: A Call to Action

Anna M. Ortiz

The authors of this volume outline the current issues facing Latinos as they work to reach their goals in higher education. Through their research and their own experiences, the authors bring to life the struggles students encounter as well as the immense pride in their accomplishments. The challenges come from all directions. González, Jovel, and Stoner (Chapter Two) outline the influence of family and of one's identity as a family member in their description of Latinas' attempts to take advantage of the best educational opportunities. Villalpando (Chapter Four), Gross (Chapter Six), and Vasquez (Chapter Seven) identify institutional structures and agents as sources of racism, discrimination, and neglect that affect students' success and satisfaction in higher education. Martinez and Fernandez (Chapter Five) remind us that the highest hurdle for Latinos is transferring from community colleges to four-year colleges and universities, a hurdle that is growing in importance, since over half of all Latino students begin their postsecondary careers at community colleges. As these barriers are explored, Torres (Chapter One) cautions that higher education researchers and student services professionals need to remember that not all Latinos are alike. Students of different Latino origins have varied histories in higher education, often as a result of the time of their immigration or their socioeconomic status both in the country of origin and in the United States.

Stories of success and support are also evident in the chapters of this volume. Juarez, Cabrales, and Mina (Chapter Seven) all speak of administrators and programs that made a difference not only in their college success but in their personal development. Dayton, Gonzalez-Vasquez, Martinez, and Plum (Chapter Three) describe institutions and administrators that are

NEW DIRECTIONS FOR STUDENT SERVICES, no. 105, Spring 2004 © Wiley Periodicals, Inc.

highly committed to Latino students. In Hispanic-serving institutions, campus culture supports students and provides opportunities to create webs of support. In Gross's chapter, an academically and professionally based student organization influenced and supported students' career aspirations and provided them with opportunities to build the efficacy necessary to make the transition from higher education to the world of work. The ethic of caring and social justice discussed by Villalpando and the widespread responsibility required of the validation team described by Martinez and Fernandez serve as guideposts for administrators and student services staff as they create campus climates in which Latinos can succeed. Through the diligent work of these authors, the following recommendations for student services professionals are made.

Learn About the History and Experiences of All Latinos

The curricula in primary and secondary education seldom include the history of Latinos in the United States beyond a cursory exploration of the groups in selected regions of the country. Therefore, most of our knowledge about the diversity among us is limited. Students take note when it is evident that we have done our homework. Knowing about the history of different groups of Latinos helps to build credibility with students and leads to a more authentic understanding of the impact of history on present circumstances. Specifically, we should know about the immigration patterns of Cubaños and other Caribbean Latinos, South Americans, Central Americans, and Mexican Americans. Each country of origin has distinct circumstances that caused the migration of its people (the push), while political, economic, and legal circumstances in the United States provided opportunities for immigration (the pull). Understanding these distinctions aids our understanding of a group's propensity for and experience with higher education (in the country of origin and in this country), socioeconomic factors that promote or inhibit higher education, and legal barriers that make participation in higher education difficult. For instance, in Chapter One, Torres shows the variances in higher education achievement for specific groups of Latinos. Strides in higher education are often a consequence of the length of time the group has been in this country (as in the case of Cubans) or the higher education experience that the group may bring from their countries of origin (as in the case of South Americans). While these are generalizations, it is important to remember that these factors vary within groups, especially with Mexican Americans and Puerto Ricans, the largest groups. Within these groups, immigration patterns have been cyclical, resulting in both new arrivals and significant numbers of group members that have been on the U.S. mainland for several generations.

To learn more about the history and immigrant experiences of Latino groups, student services professionals can take Latino studies courses, do independent reading, or participate in campus activities that focus on the cultures of these groups. The works of Alejandro Portes and his associates provide vivid descriptions and detailed demographic analyses for a variety of Latino groups. I recommend these specific volumes: *City on the Edge* (Portes and Stepick, 1993), *Immigrant America* (Portes and Rumbaut, 1996), and *Latin Journey* (Portes and Bach, 1985). Torres also recommends Florida International University's Cuban Research Institute and the Hunter College Center for Puerto Rican Studies as resources specific to these groups.

Understand the Importance and Impact of Family

In most circles, when I hear common experiences of Latinos described, the role of the family is often the first characteristic mentioned. This occurs so frequently that valuing the family as a characteristic of Latino college students borders on a stereotype. However, as the chapters in this volume demonstrate, family does play an important role in the college experience of Latino students. The family influences college choice, motivation, and integration of students into campus communities. These influences are well documented in Chapter Two. The Latinas that González, Jovel, and Stoner interviewed were torn when they decided to attend prestigious colleges far from home. Their parents tried to influence their college choice by encouraging them to attend nearby universities so that they could remain in the home. A desire for independence and the need to take full advantage of their college opportunities took these women to universities away from home. However, they discovered that being far from home took an emotional toll on them that made the process of connecting with their institution more difficult. They experienced consequences of being apart from the family environment that included their families going on without them— celebrations that they missed, new arrivals they would never know as intimately as they would if they were in closer proximity. As they approached graduation, they realized that the motivation to succeed that had been instilled through strong family experiences raised the possibility of being even farther from their families as they faced choices about graduate education. They essentially found themselves in the same situation they had faced as high school seniors.

Student services professionals who connect with Latino students often serve as institutional mediators between the home and college experiences. In Cynthia Juarez's story (Chapter Seven) three of her mentors became deeply involved with her family. At different points in Cynthia's college career, each mentor connected with her family to explain the changes in Cynthia's life and allayed their fears as she became a more independent college student who was increasingly involved in campus activities. The admission counselor whom José Cabrales worked with understood the importance of family in the college choice process. She created a program that connected José's parents to the institution and also connected other Latino parents to the university through that program. Student services professionals need to move beyond the conventional paradigm that views the student as a solitary entity that needs to be integrated into the college environment. Programs, services, and professionals that successfully work with Latino students understand that the student is part of a family system and that the family system also needs to be a part of the college experience. The student voices in Chapter Two and Chapter Three remind us that the student's family needs to be attended to in the admissions process and throughout the student's college years. Although specific recommendations for the inclusion of family in the practice of student services professionals are embedded throughout this volume, the following recommendations need to be reinforced:

• College admissions personnel can work to connect Latino parents of prospective students with parents of current Latino students. This can be done formally, through a program like the one described in José's story in Chapter Seven, or informally, through maintaining a list of parents who are willing to serve as resources in designated geographic areas. ·
• Some campuses currently include family in summer orientation programs and first-year student activities. Activities that invite and include families need to be offered throughout the undergraduate years. Student services staff can work with Latino faculty, staff, and student organizations to design these programs, or they can develop programs in which all students' families can be invited to participate.
• Although it is difficult to change the formulas for federal financial aid awards, campuses should be encouraged to include funding for trips home for students who live far away from campus. This could be accomplished by making short-term or emergency grants or loans available.
• Many campuses hold special graduation activities for Latino students. These are events at which graduates are honored and families have the opportunity to meet faculty, staff, and administrators. These kinds of events personalize graduation activities, especially in large institutions. Organizers can include first-year, sophomore, and junior students and their families in these events as a way to build community before students leave the institution.

Another aspect of the family dynamic to be considered is the generational status of the family and student. As noted in Chapter One, generational status refers to the number of generations the family has been in the United States. Lower generational status usually translates into a higher degree of connection to and participation in the culture of the country of origin. In these cases, it is more likely that the use of Spanish and other cultural characteristics are maintained. The longer the family is in the United States, the more likely it is that acculturation or assimilation into the dominant culture has occurred. Compared with families who have been in the United States for longer, the more traditional first- or second-generation families will likely have fewer experiences with higher edu-cation and stronger beliefs about preserving the culture, including adherence to traditional gender roles and deference to the expectations of elders. Differences in generational status account for significant within-group differences that need to be considered when working with Latino students.

Build Webs of Connection Among Faculty, Staff, and Students

Student services personnel who are committed to addressing the unique needs of Latino students often find themselves in effective working relationships with Latino faculty, staff, and student organizations that cross organizational structures and reporting lines. Liliana Mina's story in Chapter Seven shows that finding Latino faculty and staff across campus is important for Latino students, connecting them with the institution and providing them with needed support regardless of formal titles and duties. González, Jovel, and Stoner found that the support systems created by Latino faculty, staff, and students helped to alleviate family concerns about who would care for their daughters in the foreign environment of the university. Latino academic and Greek student organizations are also locations of support for students. Fernando Vasquez's story in Chapter Seven underscores the importance of these organizations; his Latino fraternity was where he found connection and mentoring. The students whom Gross studied in Chapter Six negotiated peer relationships and the realities of the work world in their minority business student organization. Understanding these support systems and knowing the key individuals who serve as resources for Latino students help all student services personnel to connect new students to these networks at a time they need them the most.

It would be most effective for student services personnel who are involved with first-year students to be well connected with the various individuals, services, and organizations that serve Latino students. To achieve this goal, use of the principles of good network building is in order. Frequent contact with these entities regardless of reporting lines is needed. Relationships built on reciprocity help to increase the longevity and effectiveness of the partnerships. Latino faculty, staff, and student organizations should not be used only to benefit the work of administrators, staff, and offices on campus. Whenever possible, these entities should be compensated or recognized for the instrumental role that they play. Leaders can also work to integrate these staff, services, and organizations into the mainstream structures of the university and help them negotiate the politics of the institution.

Become Aware of the Unique Impact of Racism on Latino Students

Latino critical theory challenges student affairs professionals to consider the unique impact of racism on Latino students. Villalpando explains in Chapter Four that critical race theory includes multiple dimensions of social identity as they intersect to construct unique circumstances for racism and discrimination. For instance, Latino students may face racism due to the fact that they may be phenotypically different from other students, may come from low socioeconomic backgrounds, or may speak with a Spanish accent. In addition, Latinas experience gender discrimination as they attempt to break free of stereotypes applied to them as members of a distinct cultural group. Similarly, gay or lesbian Latinos often experience additional layers of discrimination due to their sexual orientation. Despite the multiple locations of racism and discrimination, many in the college environment remain oblivious to the fact that overt and covert acts and gestures are directed at Latino students. Many of these are considered microaggressions that accumulate over time, resulting in internalized beliefs that erode students' sense of legitimacy in the college environment. Gross describes how students encountered these microaggressions in their internship environments and how they used their student organization and the friendships formed there to combat these assaults to their self-efficacy. She also outlined how students faced challenges from other Latino students who considered their involvement in business as a career and their involvement in student organizations associated with business rather than more established Latino student groups, such as MEChA, as evidence of selling out.

How can student affairs professionals assist students who are encountering racism and discrimination? A first step is to believe students when they report or suggest that they experience incivility on campus. Often we tend to minimize the importance of these events, believing that de-emphasizing them will help students feel better about themselves. Students need to know that they are heard and that staff and faculty understand the gravity of these situations. The staff then needs to become diligent about seeking out locations of covert and overt racism rather than waiting for students to bring them to their attention. These acts may be occurring in the classroom, residence halls, advisers' offices, in student government meetings or in the adjacent community. Challenging behavior, no matter how seemingly minor, helps Latino students to know that the institution is committed to creating communities where social justice and an ethic of caring are paramount. Staff can also help students to develop the defensive mechanisms necessary to prevent these acts from affecting students' self-efficacy, ambition, and ability to succeed in college. For example, the minority business association described in Chapter Six was a place where students could talk about the discrimination they encountered and where they received support from peers, staff, and even the national organization. Creating and nurturing student organizations like these are key contributions that student affairs staff can make to building more positive environments. Finally, staff and administrators can audit their own services, policies, and personnel to uncover intentional and unintentional examples of racism and discrimination. As Villalpando noted, social justice is already a philosophical foundation on which many student services professionals practice, making this recommendation a natural one through which to exert leadership on their campuses.

Include K–12 Schools and Community Colleges in a Seamless Educational Experience

Hispanic-serving institutions have been exemplary in developing partnerships with schools and communities to facilitate the access and retention of Latinos in higher education. Programs such as GEAR UP, sponsored by the W. K. Kellogg Foundation, help to build relationships, programs, and policies between four-year universities, community colleges, K-12 schools, and community organizations and agencies. While GEAR UP is a large national program, individual colleges and universities can foster relationships with community colleges, middle schools, and high schools through the use of articulation agreements, through outreach programs, and through connecting student organizations among all types of educational institutions. The programs that Martinez and Fernandez summarized in Chapter Five are excellent examples of what can be done to facilitate transfer of Latino students to four-year colleges and retention until graduation.

Obviously, this recommendation is more pertinent to student services areas such as admissions, outreach, and TRIO programs. However, the goal of a seamless educational experience should be shared by all entities on campus that wish to improve access and retention of Latino students. There are numerous ways in which diverse functional areas can reach out to community colleges, high schools, and middle schools. Career centers can offer career days, so that high school students can learn about careers that may be available to them with a college education. Residence life programs can organize overnight student visits through local community college transfer centers so that potential transfer students can experience campus life directly and witness the benefits of on-campus living. Student organizations can be encouraged to provide community service or participate in service learning programs in which they volunteer in after-school programs, tutoring and advising middle school students about college. Latino student organizations often make these types of outreach programs a regular part of their activity calendars, but other student organizations should be encouraged to participate, thus modeling that these types of efforts should be a whole-community effort. The concept of the validation team presented in Chapter Five is just as necessary in four-year institutions as in community colleges.

Focus on Experiential Learning and Building Community

If experiential education is a focus of both in-class and out-of-class learning there is great potential to make learning more relevant for students and to build community through the natural connections that experiential learning creates among all participants, whether faculty, staff, or students. The core of experiential learning from a critical race perspective, as discussed by Villalpando, is an acknowledgment that experiential knowledge is legitimate and that knowledge based on Latinos' experiences in their homes and communities is necessary and valued in the higher education community. Many Latinos already have knowledge and experiences in negotiating institutional and community structures and can traverse diverse environments to create positive change. This is evident in many chapters in this volume. When José helped to create the parent outreach program and founded the Latino fraternity on his campus, he was exercising his experiential knowledge. When this knowledge is given space for expression and subsequently valued, students build confidence, efficacy, and the skills necessary to succeed in college and beyond. The business students in Gross's chapter used their experiential knowledge in their internships and in bringing their student organization to the national level.

This recommendation reminds us that students must be a part of creating solutions and programs for their success. It would be a mistake for student affairs staff to assume that programs and services to support the success of Latino students need to be created solely by staff and administrators. Involving students in the process legitimizes what they know about their communities, families, and needs on the college campus. Given that few campuses have significant numbers of Latino faculty and staff, these students offer valuable experiences and information that can help staff to create more authentic and culturally appropriate programs and services. Latino student involvement also serves to build connections between campus constituencies and those in community colleges and K–12 schools. Student affairs staff can support students in these efforts by creating policies and procedures that encourage rather than deter student-directed programming, by serving as leadership coaches as students build the skills necessary to carry out their goals, and by providing much-needed financial and administrative support. This last point is important because many Latino student organizations not only go about the business of typical student organizations but also serve in important roles in the Latino community on and off campus.

Conclusion

The growth of the Latino student population in our colleges and universities offers our learning communities enormous potential. Latino students have much to contribute. The knowledge and experiences they bring to campus will help our institutions become not only more diverse but, I argue, more caring and responsive. In my experience, when a critical mass of Latinos enters a program or environment, new initiatives are created, new ways of organizing and leading are institutionalized, and an ethic of caring and social justice is infused. However, it is important to remember that the unique needs of Latino students require student affairs professionals to be adept in considering the holistic needs of students in ways unique to this population. Because many Latinos are first-generation college students, we often need to translate the culture of academe into frameworks that are understood by and work for Latino students. Just as we learned long ago that the head and heart cannot be separated, we also have to learn not encourage the separation of Latino students from their families and communities. We have to understand that racism and inequality have structured public education in such a way that many Latino students come to higher education less prepared but no less able. Further, we must share these understandings with our faculty and staff colleagues so that relationship-centered institutions can respond to the unique needs of all students.

References

Portes, A., and Bach, R. L. *Latin Journey: Cuban and Mexican Immigrants in the United States*. Berkeley: University of California Press, 1985.

Portes, A., and Rumbaut, R. G. *Immigrant America: A Portrait.* (2nd ed.) Berkeley: University of California Press, 1996.

Portes, A., and Stepick, A. *City on the Edge: The Transformation of Miami*. Berkeley: University of California Press, 1993.

ANNA M. ORTIZ *is associate professor of student development in higher education at California State University, Long Beach.*

INDEX

99

Back Issue/Subscription Order Form

Copy or detach and send to:
Jossey-Bass, A Wiley Imprint, 989 Market Street, San Francisco CA 94103-1741

Call or fax toll-free: Phone 888-378-2537 6:30AM – 3PM PST; Fax 888-481-2665

Back Issues: Please send me the following issues at $27 each
(Important: please include ISBN number with your order.)

_____

_____

_____

$ _____   Total for single issues

$ _____   SHIPPING CHARGES: SURFACE   Domestic Canadian
                                 First Item $5.00 $6.00
                                 Each Add'l Item $3.00 $1.50
                  For next-day and second-day delivery rates, call the number listed above.

Subscriptions   Please __ start __ renew my subscription to *New Directions for Student Services* for the year 2_____at the following rate:

U.S.	__ Individual $75	__ Institutional $160
Canada	__ Individual $75	__ Institutional $200
All Others	__ Individual $99	__ Institutional $234
Online Subscription		__ Institutional $160

**For more information about online subscriptions visit
www.interscience.wiley.com**

$ _____   Total single issues and subscriptions (Add appropriate sales tax for your state for single issue orders. No sales tax for U.S. subscriptions. Canadian residents, add GST for subscriptions and single issues.)

__Payment enclosed (U.S. check or money order only)
__VISA __ MC __ AmEx __ Card #_____Exp.Date_____

Signature _____ Day Phone _____
__Bill Me (U.S. institutional orders only. Purchase order required.)

Purchase order # _____
Federal Tax ID13559302   GST 89102 8052

Name _____

Address _____

_____

Phone _____ E-mail _____

For more information about Jossey-Bass, visit our Web site at www.josseybass.com

at making student affairs leaders more effective in their interactions with important off-campus partners, supporters, and agencies. Chapter authors explore the current challenges facing the student services profession as well as the emerging opportunities worthy of student affairs interest.
ISBN: 0-7879-6342-9

SS99   Addressing Contemporary Campus Safety Issues
Christine K. Wilkinson, James A. Rund
Provided for practitioners as a resource book for both historical and evolving issues, this guide covers hazing, parental partnerships, and collaborative relationships between universities and the neighboring community. Addressing a new definition of a safe campus environment, the editors have identified topics such as the growth in study abroad, the implications of increased usage of technology on campus, and campus response to September 11. In addition, large-scale crisis responses to student riots and multiple campus tragedies have been described in case studies. The issue speaks to a more contemporary definition of a safe campus environment that addresses not only physical safety issues but also those of a psychological nature, a more diverse student body, and quality of life.
ISBN: 0-7879-6341-0

SS98   The Art and Practical Wisdom of Student Affairs Leadership
Jon Dalton, Marguerite McClinton
This issue collects reflections, stories, and advice about the art and practice of student affairs leadership. Ten senior student affairs leaders were asked to maintain a journal and record their personal reflections on practical wisdom they have gained in the profession. The authors looked inside themselves to provide personal and candid insight into the convictions and values that have guided them in their work and lives.
ISBN: 0-7879-6340-2

SS97   Working with Asian American College Students
Marylu K. McEwen, Corinne Maekawa Kodama, Alvin N. Alvarez, Sunny Lee, Christopher T. H. Liang
Highlights the diversity of Asian American college students, analyzes the "model minority" myth and the stereotype of the "perfidious foreigner," and points out the need to consider the racial identity and racial consciousness of Asian American students. Various authors propose a model of Asian American student development, address issues of Asian Americans who are at educational risk, discuss the importance of integration and collaboration between student affairs and Asian American studies programs, and offer strategies for developing socially conscious Asian American student leaders.
ISBN: 0-7879-6292-9S

SS96   Developing External Partnerships for Cost-Effective, Enhanced Service
Larry H. Dietz, Ernest J. Enchelmayer
Offers a variety of models for the enhancement of services through external partnership, including on- and off-campus collaboration with public and private entities. Explores the challenges student affairs professionals face when determining how to meet a particular constituency's needs in the most cost-effective and efficient manner.
ISBN: 0-7879-5788-7

SS95   The Implications of Student Spirituality for Student Affairs Practice
        Margaret A. Jablonski
        Provides student affairs professionals and others on college campuses with
        information and guidance about including spirituality in student life
        programs and in the curriculum of preparation programs. Explores the role
        that faith and spirit play in individual and group development on our
        campuses. Models of leadership, staff development, and graduate education
        itself are all examined from the context of spirituality.
        ISBN: 0-7879-5787-9

SS94   Consumers, Adversaries, and Partners: Working with the Families of
        Undergraduates
        Bonnie V. Daniel, B. Ross Scott
        Presents effective strategies for student services professionals to collaborate
        and coordinate in creating a consistent message of engagement for the
        families of today's college students. Parents, stepparents, grandparents, and
        others who serve as guardians of college students are challenging
        administrators to address their concerns in a variety of areas, including
        admissions and financial aid processes, orientation programs, residence life,
        and alumni and development activities.
        ISBN: 0-7879-5786-0

SS93   Student Services for Athletes
        Mary F. Howard-Hamilton, Sherry K. Watt
        Explores a full range of issues, including the ongoing impact of Title IX, the
        integration of student athletes into on-campus residence halls, the college
        experience for minority athletes, and the expansion of opportunities for
        women athletes.
        ISBN: 0-7879-5757-7

SS92   Leadership and Management Issues for a New Century
        Dudley B. Woodard Jr., Patrick Love, Susan R. Komives
        Examines new approaches to learning requiring a new kind of leadership,
        and describes the important role played by student affairs professionals in
        creating and sustaining learning communities. Explores how changes in
        students will affect student affairs work, outlines new dimensions of student
        affairs capital, and details the importance of active and collaborative
        leadership for creating a more flexible structure to handle future challenges.
        ISBN: 0-7879-5445-4

SS91   Serving Students with Disabilities
        Holley A. Belch
        Explores the critical role that community and dignity play in creating a
        meaningful educational experience for students with disabilities and shows how
        to help these students gain meaningful access and full participation in campus
        activities. Addresses such common concerns as fulfilling legal requirements and
        overcoming architectural barriers, as well as effective approaches to recruitment
        and retention, strategies for career and academic advising, and the impact of
        financial resources on funding programs and services.
        ISBN: 0-7879-5444-6

NEW DIRECTIONS FOR STUDENT SERVICES
IS NOW AVAILABLE ONLINE AT WILEY INTERSCIENCE

What is Wiley InterScience?

Wiley InterScience is the dynamic online content service from John Wiley & Sons delivering the full text of over 300 leading scientific, technical, medical, and professional journals, plus major reference works, the acclaimed *Current Protocols* laboratory manuals, and even the full text of select Wiley print books online.

What are some special features of Wiley InterScience?

Wiley InterScience Alerts is a service that delivers table of contents via e-mail for any journal available on Wiley InterScience as soon as a new issue is published online.
Early View is Wiley's exclusive service presenting individual articles online as soon as they are ready, even before the release of the compiled print issue. These articles are complete, peer-reviewed, and citable.
CrossRef is the innovative multi-publisher reference linking system enabling readers to move seamlessly from a reference in a journal article to the cited publication, typically located on a different server and published by a different publisher.

How can I access Wiley InterScience?

Visit http://www.interscience.wiley.com

Guest Users can browse Wiley InterScience for unrestricted access to journal Tables of Contents and Article Abstracts, or use the powerful search engine.
Registered Users are provided with a *Personal Home Page* to store and manage customized alerts, searches, and links to favorite journals and articles. Additionally, Registered Users can view free Online Sample Issues and preview selected material from major reference works.
Licensed Customers are entitled to access full-text journal articles in PDF, with select journals also offering full-text HTML.

How do I become an Authorized User?

Authorized Users are individuals authorized by a paying Customer to have access to the journals in Wiley InterScience. For example, a university that subscribes to Wiley journals is considered to be the Customer. Faculty, staff and students authorized by the university to have access to those journals in Wiley InterScience are Authorized Users. Users should contact their Library for information on which Wiley journals they have access to in Wiley InterScience.

ASK YOUR INSTITUTION ABOUT WILEY INTERSCIENCE TODAY!